AF663349

STOCK LINGUA

STOCK LINGUA

COMMON SENSE INVESTING

Pankaj Singhania

Vitasta

To the Indian Armed Forces for being a pillar of strength to our great nation. You continue to safeguard our frontiers.

Published by
Renu Kaul Verma
Vitasta Publishing Pvt Ltd
2/15, Ansari Road, Daryaganj
New Delhi - 110 002
info@vitastapublishing.com

ISBN: 978-93-90961-88-7
© Pankaj Singhania
First Edition 2023
MRP ₹450

All Rights Reserved.
No part of this publication may be reproduced, stored in a retrieval system, or transmitted in any form, or by any means—electronic, mechanical, photocopying, recording or otherwise—without the prior permission of the publisher. Opinions expressed in this book are the author's own. The publisher is in no way responsible for these.

Edited by Sangita Menon Malhan
Typeset & Cover Design by Somesh Kumar Mishra
Printed by Vikas Computer and Printers, New Delhi

Contents

Chapter 1

TO INVEST OR NOT?

Vikram was caught in the cleft between a sneaking worry and genuine happiness. It was his son's first day at school. After quite a struggle, he and his wife had succeeded in getting their son admitted to kindergarten in one of the better known schools in the city. It would soon be time for their younger child, their one and a half-year-old daughter, to begin her formal education.

Vikram's job at a consulting firm paid him well enough to live a comfortable life in a tier I city, but not enough to fulfil his aspirations. Financially, there was little contribution from his wife, Sandhya, whose earnings from following her passion for baking, were sporadic, and barely made up for her investment.

Sandhya and Vikram were in their early thirties, and lived in a rented apartment in one of the high rise condominiums, known for its amenities for the residents. His parents lived a retired life in his hometown, and sometimes, Vikram also had to take on their financial requirements.

The thought that worried him was that his financial commitments had already overtaken his means. There wasn't much in the name of savings or investments other than some money he had put aside as a fixed deposit and some retirement benefit policies he had bought, hoping that these would grow in time to allow him to fulfil some of his long term plans. The problem was that these were not growing fast enough. Driven by some of his colleagues, he had dabbled in the stock market, but quit quickly after losing money. The stock market was something he couldn't figure out, even with all the available free advice.

Vikram was at a loss. How on earth was he

going to pay for his four bedroom flat, meet the higher education expenses of his children, running into lakhs of rupees, and still go on to meet his aspirations of buying a bigger car, go on vacations abroad, and not let his parents down in terms of financial help? His salary, increasing at 10-15 per cent every year, would clearly not suffice.

With rising inflation and expenses running greater than wages, do you feel the same as Vikram? If yes, what are you doing to tackle the situation?

'What's troubling you, young man?' Vikram's boss asked him, startling him in the process.

'I have noticed that you've been lost for the past few days,' he said. Vikram smiled politely.

He wished he could have confessed that he wasn't daydreaming—that he was plagued with worry. Then, it struck him. He ought to speak to his boss, Rohan, who was in his early 30s. Rohan was doing very well, both professionally and personally. Moreover, he had gained quite a reputation as a man who played the stock market well. Vikram was reasonably close to Rohan, having graduated from the same management institute.

'Rohan, I need some advice from you,' Vikram confessed.

'Sure! What about? Not happy with the work?' Rohan's eyebrows furrowed. 'Planning a move?' he probed.

'Oh, no! Nothing like that. This is something personal,' assured Vikram.

'Okay, then. Join me for lunch and drinks over the weekend. My family is away, and we can talk freely,' he offered.

'That is great. See you soon,' Vikram replied. He was relieved.

'How do I grow my money, boss?' Vikram threw the question directly at Rohan without beating around the bush, once they were done with lunch. It was a lazy Saturday afternoon in Rohan's five-bedroom apartment in one of the signature high rises in the city. No one was in a hurry.

Taken aback by the directness of the question, Rohan stared at Vikram for a couple of minutes, and then smiled. 'Ah! So that is what has been bothering you,' he responded.

'Look, brother! Money won't grow on its own. Even that ornamental creeper called Money Plant doesn't grow if you don't provide it with the means to grow. So, tell me about everything that you have done so far to make your money grow,' entreated Vikram.

Rohan heard attentively about Vikram's savings, fixed deposits, investments in retirement policy plans and his failed attempts at the stock market, and shook his head.

'From what I can gather, you have made the same mistakes that most people make. **I will have to take you through the basics of**

savings and investment before I explain the more complicated stuff. Don't worry! I won't make it a dry and boring lecture. But you cannot be impatient because there is no magic shortcut to grow money,' he cautioned.

The learning began. Vikram could see that Rohan was genuinely concerned about his amateurish approach. He wasn't too happy about being lectured either, but then, Rohan was someone who had burnt his hands in the fire and come out with a winning formula. Therefore, it was better to listen to what he was saying, setting aside all ego.

'Let's get the very basic stuff out of the way first. If you think your money will increase by putting it in a savings account or a fixed deposit, think hard,' began Rohan.

'With inflation at five per cent, eating into the value of money, your money in the savings account is barely growing at one per cent every year. The interest rate paid by the bank on your fixed deposit may be a little higher, but after accounting for inflation, don't forget that you have to pay a tax on the amount that you earn

Have you ever considered investing in stocks?

on interest. In short, in both cases, the growth is only nominal. Nowhere close to what you need,' he pointed out.

'What about the retirement and pension plans where I have invested?' asked Vikram. He wanted clarity.

'Probably better than the two points we just discussed, but you need to remember three things when evaluating them vis-à-vis your needs. First, is your investment large enough to give you financial security after you turn sixty. Second, you will have to pay a tax on a substantial amount of what you get after the plan matures. Third, and in my opinion, most important, the stocks where your money is invested are chosen by people who don't know you or your needs. You can tell them whether to invest in debt, equity or government bonds, but you cannot choose the stocks for them. And last, but not the least, don't forget to adjust

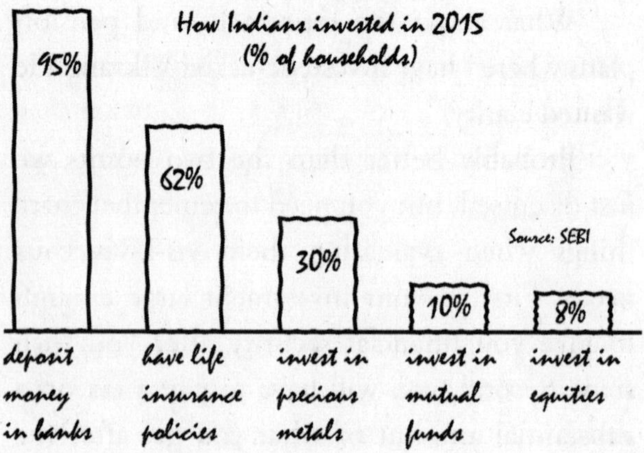
How Indians invested in 2015
(% of households)
95%
62%
30%
10%
8%
Source: SEBI
deposit money in banks
have life insurance policies
invest in precious metals
invest in mutual funds
invest in equities

the final returns to inflation. One or two crore rupees might sound a lot today, but that may not be the case in twenty years, when you are likely to get the invested money back,' Rohan noted sharply.

'What do you suggest I do then?' asked Vikram.

'Before I tell you, let me give you the big picture of how we Indians manage our money. That will make it easier for you to put what I tell you thereafter in the right context,' Rohan said. Reaching for his MacBook Air, he opened a report.

'Do you know what a small percentage of Indians invest in or are even aware of stock market investment? Here is a survey of about 50,000 households conducted by the Securities and Exchange Board of India (SEBI) in 2015,' he said, showing the report to Vikram.

'Against 99.9 per cent respondents being aware of bank savings, only 26.3 per cent were aware of investment in equities. The difference becomes starker when we move from awareness to actual practice. While 95 per cent urban respondents deposit money in banks, just about 10 per cent and 8 per cent invest in mutual funds and equities, respectively,' Rohan elucidated.

'The survey found that a third of the households shy away from investing in mutual funds, and a quarter from the equities because they are not sure about the safety of such investments. In the case of equities, over a fifth of households is held back by the lack of adequate information, and a significant share of households is apprehensive that this lack of expertise might lead to losses,' Rohan pointed out.

'That's a pretty gloomy picture!' Vikram interjected.

'Quite so! But things are changing as more people move to urban areas and start earning more. They are looking for avenues to multiply the rate of increasing their wealth. And, in that pursuit of wealth, more people are flocking to the stock market. The attraction and the temptation generated by "rags to riches" stories become irresistible,' Rohan noted.

'But surely not all of them are making a lot of money? Who can predict when the market will tank, wiping away the investments of so many people! That's how I lost so much, and quit the market as a result, Vikram recalled. He couldn't forget the pain of losing a few lakhs within no time.

'We will come to the part of making money a little later. Let me first answer your question about the losses you made. The basic principle you need to remember here is that no one can stop Mr Market in the long run. Let me give you the example of how the market reacted to the COVID epidemic,' declared Rohan.

'As the Corona virus pandemic hit the world, stock markets witnessed a sharp decline.

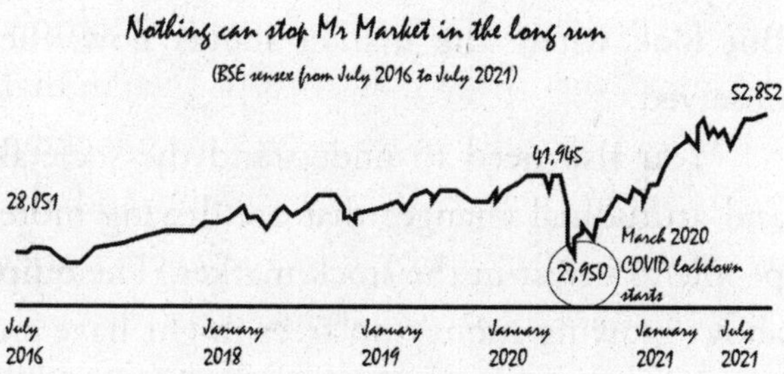

And, as is the case with black swan events, the world was not prepared for it. A leading stock market magazine in India had made the editorial proclamation in December 2019, "Year 2020 to be high on steroids," predicting a broad based rise of the stock market, a lot of reforms, and government doles to push the economy to a higher orbit. Stock markets across the world were gasping for breath within the next three months. Governments pumped in money, but only to keep the economy afloat. "Stock market investors lose Rs 46 lakh crore [trillion] in 38 sessions," between January and mid-March 2020, reported the *Economic Times*. Many such stories of crippling losses contribute to the folktales of the stock market. But look where the market stands now,' he observed.

'You also need to understand the societal and attitudinal changes that are driving more people to invest in the stock market. The quip about growing money on trees might have an air of sarcasm about it, but many of us have, at some point, secretly wished it to be true. The age-old caution of cutting our coat according to the cloth is now passé. We are borrowing more. Financial liabilities of households in the current decade have grown faster than savings. But more importantly, we strive to acquire more cloth, and faster. This change in this particular societal philosophy is reflected in a gradual transition from a preference for protecting money to growing it, for which the preferred route is investment in shares and debentures. All you have to do to feel this change is to look at the phenomenal growth in the number of dematerialised accounts in our country in the past decade,' Rohan insisted.

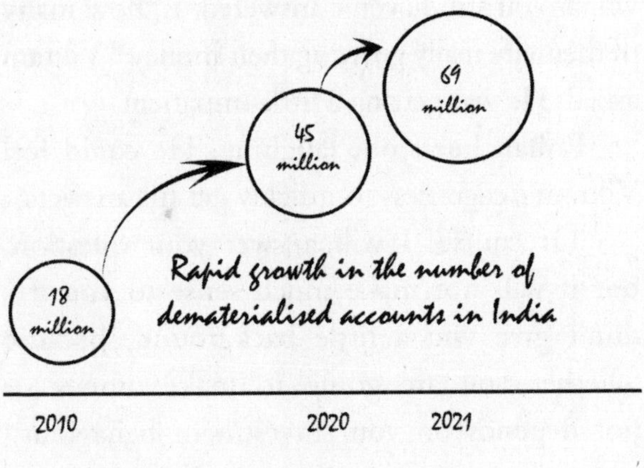

'This also reflects a shift to the risk-taking attitude of the youth. Out of the 27 million new dematerialised accounts added between 2010 and 2020, 2.4 million, or nearly a tenth was added in just three months between March and June 2020. A tanked stock market, due to the onset of the COVID-19 pandemic, certainly provided an attractive environment for buying stocks. Yet, the surge in the number of new investors is a perfect pointer that more people, especially the youth, are eager to take risks to grow their money,' he noted.

'So, you are telling me that more people are investing in the stock market? But my question, which you still haven't answered, is, how many of them are really growing their money?' Vikram asked. He was getting a little impatient.

Rohan burst out laughing. He could feel Vikram's eagerness to quickly get his answers.

'Of course, I will answer your question, but it will not make much sense to you if I don't give you a little background, because whether you are going to make money or not depends on your investment behaviour,'

What is your investment behaviour? Do you agree with Rohan?

Rohan remarked, and smiled. 'Remember your own behaviour? You invested some money, lost it, and quickly moved out to prevent further losses. Keep that in mind while I explain this next part,' he asserted.

'In July 2020, Jay Clayton, the head of the US Securities and Exchange Commission (SEC) told CNBC that the SEC was noticing significant inflows from retail investors that have the hallmarks of short-term inflows,' he stated.

'What's the problem with that?' Vikram asked.

'The problem is that such short term trades

Stocks???
Retirement Plan???
Savings account?? FD???
Mutual Funds???

• Long Term?
• Short Selling?
• Stop Loss?
• Market Profit/Loss?

typically are high risk for those putting in their money with the aim of getting rich quickly. "Making as much money as quickly as possible" is not an investment strategy. Unfortunately, for most small investors, that is the strategy. A rise in that trend was what worried Clayton. It is a good reason for any market authority to worry, but that's not the only concern. Retail investors in the stock market are often found to put themselves at risk for a variety of reasons, based on erratic decisions. Let me show you another study,' offered Rohan. He asked Vikram to look at the screen of his MacBook Air.

'A study of investment patterns in BSE500 stocks between March 2017 and June 2018 revealed that retail investors consistently favoured stocks which yielded lower returns than the BSE500 average during the period. To make matters worse, they were found to sell stocks with higher returns than the BSE500 average. In contrast, the institutional investors increased their stake in stocks that yielded 3.2 times the average BSE500 returns during these fifteen months. In other words, although they were losing money, the small investors were unable to identify and switch over to higher yielding stocks. The CEO of a firm that offers broking services to retail investors blamed them for their lack of understanding of the intricacies of investment and their keenness for quick returns. "Without thorough knowledge, they end up investing in high beta stocks" he had said,' articulated Rohan.

'The CEO is right. Yet, in diagnosing one problem, he had unknowingly demonstrated a few more, which pose bigger challenges to retail investors making the correct decisions. The easy reference to beta stocks indicates

> *Alpha measures the amount that the investment has returned in comparison to the market index or other broad benchmark that it is compared against.*
>
> *Beta measures the relative volatility of an investment. It is an indication of its relative risk.*
>
> *Source: Investopedia*

the pervasive use of technical jargon in the matter of investments that more often than not become impediments to retail investors. The usage of the terms—alpha and beta stocks, in effect, creates sweeping generalised perceptions of infallibility in the judgement of stock performance, just as phrases like bull run and bear phase do. Sure, expert investors dive deep into technical analysis, looking for that perfect predictor of market turns. But most of us don't have a Ph.D. in economics, and simply look for maximum returns with minimum time spent,' he lamented.

'A bull run tends to lead retail investors to imagine that all the companies listed in the exchange, across sectors, have suddenly started performing well. It becomes a sort of hysteria, where we suddenly turn exuberantly optimistic. Similarly, a bear phase creates the perception among ordinary investors that all companies are performing equally badly. These perceptions are far from reality. Such a state of frenzy has been made memorable by the phrase "irrational exuberance," reportedly

WHERE RETAIL INVESTORS GO WRONG

- CONFIRMATION BIAS: Investors act upon information that they want to hear and ignore unfamiliar information.
- AVAILABILITY BIAS: Investors trust familiar information without going deeper into the source and nature of the information.
- HERD BEHAVIOUR: Individual investors tend to follow what other retail investors are doing.

coined by Robert J Shiller, professor at the Yale University, and famously used by Alan Greenspan, former chairman of the US Federal Reserve,' he noted.

'You mean jargon should be avoided?' Vikram asked. He was puzzled. 'But almost all successful investors depend on the assessment of technicalities! And, if one is not familiar with technical terms, how can one compete with them?' Vikram argued.

'Oh no! I don't mean that you should not know the jargon. All I am saying is that you cannot make your decision driven by complex technicalities that stock market experts keep throwing at you,' Rohan responded. 'Think of the term irrational exuberance, which Greenspan used. People started responding to the developments in the market without really understanding what was going on. The other side of it is irrational panic. One of the biggest drawbacks of being influenced by jargon is that you tend to develop various sorts of biases like "confirmation bias" and "availability bias," which can be harmful for your investment decision,' he stressed.

'Have you heard of Maxime Merli and Tristan Roger?' Rohan asked.

'No, I haven't. What about them?' replied Vikram.

'They are researchers at the Strasbourg Business School in France. They demonstrated that individual investors exhibit the attribute of following the crowd – known as "herding" in technical jargon – more than institutional investors. However, they also found that sophisticated investors are less prone to herding, and those who invest differently from the crowd tend to perform better by reallocating their portfolio,' Rohan pointed out.

'Yes, I vaguely remember reading a report about this,' confirmed Vikram, trying to recall it. 'Ah yes! Got it! During the bull run in 2017-18, it was reported that the portfolio returns of retail investors were not reflecting the rise in benchmark indices. While the markets soared to new heights, the holding value of retail investors in BSE200 companies actually dropped by 7 per cent. The anomaly was explained by the fact that the rise in the indices was driven only by a limited number of stocks. Those who chose the right stocks were making money, and those who didn't were on the losing side,' he remarked.

'Correct! That means a lot of retail investors were choosing the same or similar stocks which were not yielding higher returns. There's another example that I came across in the newspapers,' Rohan pointed out. 'Credit Suisse explained that the top ten contributing stocks in Nifty accounted for 218 per cent of the growth since 2015, while the bottom ten accounted for a 95 per cent decline. This means that retail investors stand to lose money or get less returns even in a bull run,' he added.

'In other words, making decisions based on averages can mostly lead to unforeseen risks. As Nassim Nicholas Taleb, author of acclaimed books like *The Black Swan* and *Skin in the Game* put it succinctly, "never cross a river if it is on average four feet deep". That kind of information fails to tell you where the river is six feet deep and where it is only two feet. The example can be extended to point out the fact that technical information is not always enough, even if it appears to makes sense on the face of it. Common sense dictates that there will be points where the depth of the river will be far more than four feet, making the chances of drowning very real,' cautioned Rohan.

'But why harp so much on the understanding and knowledge of the investor? In any case, he normally gets expert advice from his broker or fund manager!' retorted Vikram. He sounded exasperated.

'Well, yes and no,' countered Rohan. 'Indian investors display puzzling behaviour. Although 75 per cent have a running account with financial intermediaries, when it comes to making an investment decision, 43 per cent trust their own judgement, and another 16 per cent put faith in what friends and family members may have suggested. This assumes critical importance when you take into account the fact that 45 per cent of trades in stock markets, as in the NSE, are accounted for by individual investors,' remarked Rohan.

'The good news is that myriad stock

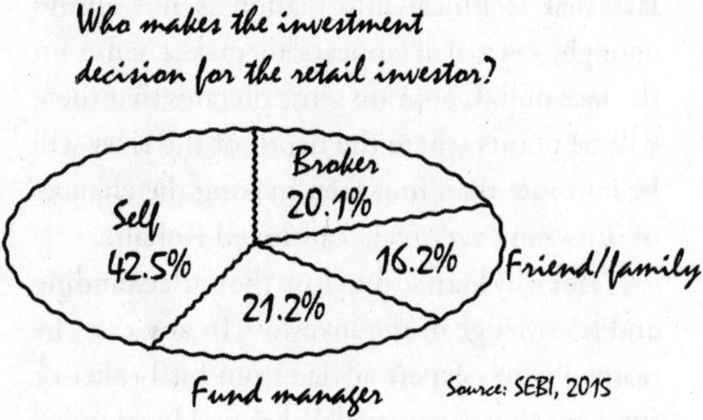

market gurus try to grab your attention, and tell you how to make money. The challenging part is that most will expect you to dive into technicalities and understand complicated formulas. They will insist that this is essential to make sense of where the stock market is going. They assume that as a lay investor, you will have the time and scope to comprehend these complex technicalities. In fact, jargon, charts and formulas have become so pervasive that you may not believe me when I insist that you can just simply rely on your common sense and some additional basic information to become a successful investor,' Rohan proclaimed. He then got up to get some beer.

Vikram opened the can, but before taking a sip, he shot out a question. The discussion was getting too interesting to be interrupted. 'You seriously mean that I can do without all that technical analysis, financial evaluation and other highfalutin stuff that brokers and fund managers usually rattle off? Seriously, I can't buy this. It seems like oversimplification,' he said, provocatively.

'I knew you wouldn't believe me,' replied Rohan. He had that "I-told-you-so" smile. 'In that case, let me tell you the story of Keith Lee. No less than Forbes published his mind-boggling achievement,' he remarked.

'Brown Capital in Baltimore, USA, which is headed by Keith Lee has 12 billion dollars in assets. Its unique characteristic is that it hunts for unglamorous but fast growing companies. It prefers companies that have revenues of less than 250 million dollars. When the market was going down in 2019, Brown's flagship Small Company Fund rose to beat the market, going up 21 per cent. The fund has averaged a 19 per cent return annually over the past decade. Since its inception in 1992, the fund is up twenty-two fold. Just how much number-crunching and chart analysis do you think was needed for that kind of performance? "I wish I could sit here and tell you that we have all these incredible algorithms and a very sophisticated way. But it really is just fundamental research," Lee had revealed. Surprising. Isn't it? Do you see what I mean?' prodded Rohan.

He continued, 'Being limited by technical information and losing out on the larger picture of business fundamentals is perhaps best exemplified by the story of the hot dog seller and his son. This story, which has developed into a sort of a business parable is so popular that there are several versions that vary in detail, and it is practically impossible to find out how or from where it originated.

The story goes thus:

A man had set up a roadside hot dog stand. He paid great attention to the quality of the meat and the buns. He offered a variety of the finest meats, and he used only freshly baked buns. Fresh accompaniments and sauces added to the taste that customers loved. The man kept the place squeaky clean, greeted customers with a smile, was prompt in his service, and treated the gradually recruited helping staff with due respect, rewarding them for their good work. Great food and positive vibes turned his stand into a centre of attraction. It became extremely popular, and people started flocking to it even from faraway places. Soon, his hot dog stand became a feature for tourists, too.

Before long, the man made enough money to send his son to a good college. After doing very well in his studies, the son landed a management job. He also wanted to help his father improve his business. As far as the man was concerned, business was already good. Yet, presuming that with a college degree, his son must have better knowledge of how to grow a business, he accepted some of his son's suggestions.

The first of those was to improve the margin by cutting costs. This, the son recommended, was to be done by selling slightly lower quality hot dogs. The margin improved, but the older man noticed a drop in sales. The son, thereafter, recommended an increase in the price of the hot dogs to offset the fall in sales. Sales dropped further. The next piece of advice from the son was to reduce staff to reduce manpower costs. Fewer customers and lower sales did not warrant the same workforce as before, he argued. Gradually, in the hope of improving margins, the man gave up on the homemade condiments and fresh buns. Cheaper options were outsourced. Portion size was also reduced. The lack of workforce also impacted the quality of service and the cleanliness of the place. The buzz of enthusiasm and positivity slowly vanished.

Letting go of one thing after another – things that added to the value of the hot dog stand – took the man back to the early stages of his business. Only now, it had none of the features that drew in the crowds in the first place.

If the moral of the story can be summed up in one sentence, it is that *decisions based on technical knowledge that make apparent business*

Do you think one should rely on common sense while making Investment decisions?

sense can go wrong if the fundamentals of a business are ignored,' stressed Rohan.

'What's your point?' prodded Vikram.

'My point is that just as in running a business, growing an investment in the stock market also depends on some fundamental principles, which are more common sense based than technical. And this starts with how one views the stock market,' claimed Rohan.

'Of course, a stock exchange has a technical definition. Simply put, it is the market place where people buy and sell stocks, bonds and commodities. This market place, like any other, provides the opportunity to trade assets for making profits. All this is true. But is that all?' he demanded.

'What else can it be? I buy stocks and I sell them when I see an opportunity to book profits,' replied Vikram wryly. He couldn't comprehend the (deeper) philosophy that Rohan seemed to be offering.

'Sure, but there's much more,' responded Rohan. 'And, that understanding is the first step while forming your investment strategy, that will lead you to great wealth. Stop for a moment. Look beyond the obvious. Beneath all the noise and rush lies the most fundamental truth that we almost always forget or tend to overlook. The stock market allows us to become partners in companies and business leaders,' proclaimed Rohan.

'What?' retorted Vikram sharply.

'Sounds absurd? Let me make it simple,' replied Rohan, rather calmly. 'Imagine yourself walking into the office of a large corporation and requesting the CEO to make you a partner in the business. I leave the reaction to your imagination. It can be anything but approval. It is highly unlikely that you will make it past the reception with such a request. Yet, that is exactly what your investment in buying shares of a company allows you to do. You become a partner,' explained Rohan.

'Ah! Now I see your point,' said Vikram, nodding. 'I will then have a team of professionals who are taking care of everything required to run the business successfully, whose only interest lies in making my money grow at the fastest possible pace. I don't have to bother about its day to day decision making. I will have a share in its profits, and, on top of that, I'll have the opportunity to voice my opinion to the management, although in a limited sphere. Above all, if I am not happy with the way the business is being run, I can just walk away, and acquire a partnership in another company,' he declared.

'Exactly!' said Rohan, and clapped. 'That is what I call the partnership model of stock

TRADING IS ONLY AN ACTIVITY
IN THE STOCK MARKET.

Think deeper.

INVESTING IN A COMPANY
MAKES YOU A PARTNER
IN THEIR GROWTH STORY.

market investment. Once you start viewing acquisition of shares in the stock market from this partnership model, a whole new avenue opens up in terms of investment strategy. It provides unique clarity on the most basic questions that confound retail investors,' he pointed out.

'Sounds fantastic, Rohan, but how does one decide where to invest?' probed Vikram. His curiosity had been piqued.

'Good question! Let's start at the beginning,' suggested Rohan.

'Keeping aside trend or technical analysis or inputs from analysts and advisers, answering this question should be simple for you as the person who is going to put money into a business. Tell me, would you want to be a partner in a business that is a trusted one, considered among the best with proven business acumen and a promising future, or partner with an unknown company?' he asked.

'The answer is obvious!' shot back Vikram.

'Precisely! If you tell me that you have one lakh rupees and that you want to be a partner with Ratan Tata or that you want to buy a bank or own oil fields, or that you want a share in every rupee earned by Nestlé and also directly question its management for their decisions, I want to tell you that it is perfectly possible. The stock exchange makes this possible,' Rohan said, with visible conviction.

Vikram wasn't happy. 'Well, as a matter of general principle, that sounds fine, but it doesn't really tell me how to select a profitable company. They come in all shapes and sizes and in so many sectors and sub sectors. I need more specific inputs to be able to sift through more than seven thousand companies currently listed on the Bombay and the National Stock Exchanges,' he argued.

'That's a fair point. Many of my friends often ask me whether it wouldn't be better to put their money in smaller companies, relatively unknown but showing signs of fast growth. It is a common perception bias that smaller companies, especially in the digital space, are more flexible to respond to market challenges by quickly changing course and being quick in innovation. So, the question here is, are large, established corporations being increasingly displaced by new technologies, or whether they are actually leveraging digital and other new technologies to innovate and grow?' asked Rohan.

'That's a tough one to answer,' admitted Vikram. He was trying find an answer. Rohan, however, continued.

What are Large and Small Cap companies?

He said, 'This notion that large companies are slow to innovate and that their business will soon be disrupted by small firms goes against research findings, which show that large companies are thriving, and that they are investing in innovation and intangible assets at an increasing pace. This, while the investment and growth opportunity of small companies is shrinking, with their nimbleness and grit increasingly under pressure.'

'You see, in the stock market, small is not always beautiful. A study by the *Harvard Business Review* (HBR) shows that the difference in median returns on operating assets has actually widened between large cap and small cap companies over a period of time. This difference between the two was 15 per cent in the 1990s but has since doubled to 30 to 35 per cent. Large companies are getting more profitable, whereas smaller ones are suffering from persistent unprofitability. While around 10-15 per cent of large cap companies reported annual losses in recent years, the share is as high as 60-65 per cent for the small companies. The main driver, which has caused this divergence between the small cap and large cap industries, also happens to be a key factor of enterprise performance and growth—the rate of investment in tangible and intangible assets. This can be investments into research and development, brands, technology or human resources. There has been a dramatic increase in the gap between how much large caps and small caps invest in these intangibles,' he continued.

'This phenomenon was observed in India, too, in 2018, at a time when more than half of the listed companies were down by over 50 per cent. While the broader markets underperformed by a huge margin, select large cap stocks got the key benchmark indices in the green, and as a result, dominated the market's performance. The stability and better long term performance of the large cap and mid cap companies have led many experienced equity investors to form about three fourths of their portfolio. A significant number of them don't invest in stocks with less than Rs thousand crore market capitalisation, and have found

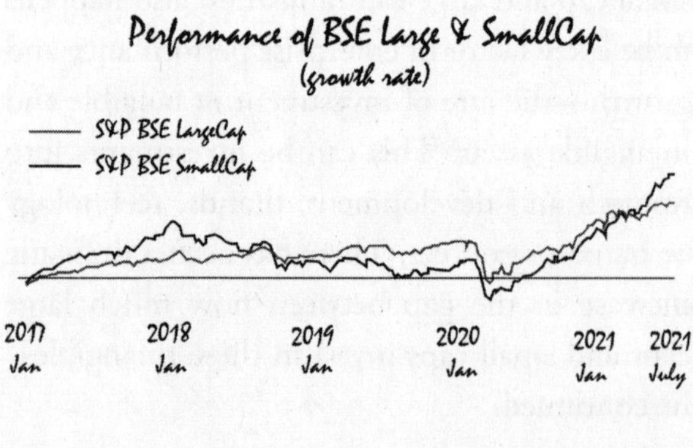

their strategy working well for them. There is a set of investors, though, that believes there is value emerging in the mid-caps and small caps. However, I see that even those investors allocate a larger share of their investments in large caps. Certainly, there will be variations year on year, but aren't we talking about a long term strategy here? There are, of course, several large cap stocks that struggle to remain in the positive territory even as the Sensex comes within kissing distance of its all-time high. That only highlights the argument that I am making – the size of market cap is only an indicator. It cannot be the sole decider of choosing a stock. This particular phenomenon underscores that the surge in the indices is not broad based. All the more reason that we should weigh in other factors before jumping in,' Rohan stressed.

Vikram looked confused. Everything Rohan had told him over the past couple of hours made a lot of sense, but it still didn't answer his central question of how to make his money grow. How would he know which companies to choose and which ones to avoid?

'I know, Vikram. I know,' confessed Rohan, as if he could read his interlocutor's mind. 'There are still way too many unanswered questions. Today was just a warm up. But do not think that everything I have said today was random rambling. I have only laid down the groundwork for the next round of our discussions,' he assured. 'I am going to let you into a little secret of mine. All my investment decisions are guided by a framework of filters which I have developed on the basis of many years of experience,' he declared. 'It is what you call the "Chef's secret recipe". I am going to share that recipe with you, and take you through each filter, explaining the purpose it serves. But before that, I am going to ask you to "know thyself",' he said, rather curiously.

The markets explained

- The majority of market news is irrelevant.
- Not a single person in the world knows what will happen in the market in the short run.
- What happens in the markets on a daily basis is overwhelmingly driven by random chance. Ascribing explanations to short-term moves is like trying to explain lottery results.
- The phrase 'double-dip recession' was mentioned 10.8 million times in 2010-11. It never came. There was virtually no mention of 'financial collapse' in 2006-07. Yet, it did happen.
- Markets go through one big pullback every year, and one massive pullback every decade.

Chapter 2

KNOW THYSELF

The discussion at Rohan's place had stopped abruptly but on a tantalising note. Vikram couldn't stop thinking about it. What did Rohan mean by "know thyself" he wondered. "I know myself well! I know everything I want from life, and I know my impending financial demands and pressures," he thought to himself. "The only thing that I do not know yet is how to grow my money to meet all those needs." These thoughts continued to occupy him.

As he was winding up work on Friday evening, and looking forward to a weekend undisturbed by sudden and unforeseen projects,

Vikram saw Rohan step out of his cabin at the far end of the hall.

'Off, busy boy?' Rohan asked from a distance, and walked briskly towards him. Vikram shut his eyes briefly, feverishly hoping that no assignment would come his way. He disliked unscheduled work getting in the way of his leisure hours.

Thankfully, that wasn't the case. Rohan slapped Vikram's back and smiled. 'You owe me a few drinks for sure. After all, the wisdom I shared with you was gratis,' he said, teasingly.

'Sure, boss. Why not? That will give me another chance to pick your brains, and to coax you to solve the riddle,' replied Vikram, and laughed.

'Nah! This is going to be pure payback,' retorted Rohan. He appeared to be in a good mood. 'I have to reach home to spend time with the family. They are back in town. But I don't mind unwinding for an hour before I reach home. So, I am offering you the chance to pay up your debt,' he declared.

Pubs and restaurants on Friday evenings

may not be conducive for serious discussions. The loud music and the chattering crowds allow no scope for a coherent conversation. But Rohan and Vikram settled down at a corner table at one of the microbreweries, and ordered their favourite drinks.

Vikram was sure that Rohan wasn't going to take up the discussion on investment decision anytime soon. At least not so soon after their marathon session over the weekend. They discussed work and also exchanged some office gossip.

Their second round of drinks nearly finished, Rohan suddenly looked up, and asked Vikram, 'Ever heard of the name Grace Groner?'

Vikram was taken aback. Where was this coming from? Some new partner joining the firm? All he could do was shake his head, a bit confused.

Rohan started speaking.

'Grace Groner was orphaned at age twelve. She never married. She never had children. She never drove a car. She lived most of her life alone in a one-bedroom house, and worked her whole career as a secretary. She was, by all accounts, a lovely lady. But she lived a humble life. That made the 7 million US Dollars she left to charity after her death in 2010 at age 100 all the more intriguing. People who knew her asked: How and from where did Grace get all that money?'

Vikram could sense where this was going, but he was still not completely sure.

'Gradually, it came to light that Grace had purchased three shares worth sixty dollars each in Abbott Laboratories, where she had also worked for over four decades,' Rohan continued with an enigmatic smile. 'She held on to those shares and reinvested the dividends each time. The shares had split so many times since 1935 when she had bought them, that in 2010, she owned 100,000 shares worth more than 7 million dollars. This mindboggling amount was the result of uninterrupted compounding in the stock market,' he elaborated.

In other words, there was no secret. There was no inheritance. Grace took her humble

> Compounding is the process in which an asset's earnings, from either capital gains or interest, are reinvested to generate additional earnings over time. This growth, calculated using exponential functions, occurs because the investment will generate earnings from both its initial principal and the accumulated earnings from preceding periods.
>
> Source: Investopedia

savings from a meagre salary and enjoyed eighty years of hands off compounding in the stock market. That was it.

'The point being?' Vikram was still trying to understand.

'Two points. First, the story demonstrates the benefits of choosing a good company; one that grows steadily. Second, the power of compounding. If you can invest and hold in a growth company, it will be a variant of a rags to riches story. These two things happened with Grace. And, do you know what? There's a third point, too. Grace had no technical knowledge about the stock market,' Rohan declared.

'Let me give you another example. Not an individual this time, but a financial firm. NatWest Markets had invested Rs 40 crore for a 20 per cent stake in the HDFC Bank in 1995. When NatWest started considering selling its stake in 2013, the value of that stake had gone up to Rs 270 crore,' he disclosed.

'Point taken. But what happens if I don't follow these lessons?' Vikram asked, trying to provoke Rohan.

'Hmmm. Let me tell you another story then. The story of Richard Fuscone.' Rohan refused to take the bait.

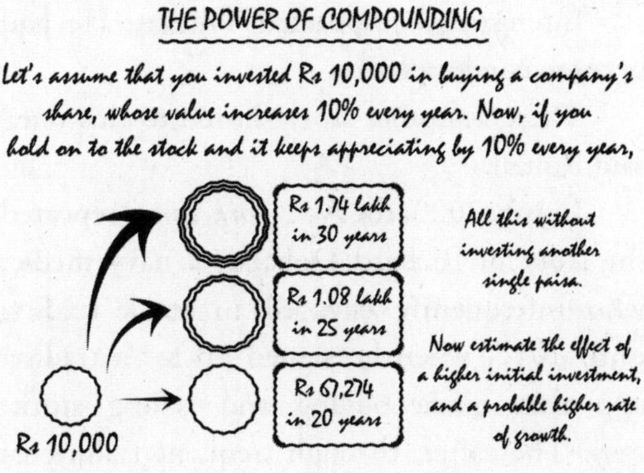

'Richard Fuscone's story stands in stark contrast to Grace Groner's. Educated at Harvard and at the University of Chicago, Richard made rapid strides in his career, becoming the vice chairman of Merrill Lynch's Latin America division. A dream run in the investment industry led him to retire in his forties. But heavy borrowing and illiquid investments led him to declare bankruptcy, striving to stave off foreclosure on his two palatial houses. A man with all the required knowledge and wherewithal to succeed fabulously in the stock market turned out to be a colossal failure,' he revealed.

'Interesting,' responded Vikram. He had become contemplative.

'There's another story. Listen to this one,' said Rohan.

'In July 2020, the *New York Times* reported the story of Richard Dobatse, a navy medic, who infrequently engaged in stock trading until 2017, when he signed up for a trading app that made buying and selling stocks easy. Thereafter, through frequent trading of speculative stocks, his initial credit funded investment of 15,000 dollars, his account value rocketed to a million dollars by 2020. He had also taken two 30,000 dollars' home equity loans to fund his trading activity. However, by July 2020, his balance had declined to 6,956 dollars – dented by the repeated losses he had to face due to his frequent trades in the hope of shoring up his fortune,' he narrated.

'The stories of Grace Groner and Richard Fuscone underscore the point you made during our last discussion. Success in stock market investing is not a function of technical knowledge,' admitted Vikram.

'Precisely!' retorted Rohan. 'But all three stories also illustrate another fundamental aspect of investing, one which we often tend to ignore: the philosophy of investing. Or, the mindset of the investor. These stories describe three entirely different mindsets. While Grace left her investments undisturbed for a long time, reinvesting the gains, Richard Fuscone sought to take his success to another level, and Richard Dobatse overplayed his hand in order to climb the ladder in a tearing hurry, thus miscounting the steps. Their attitudes and their philosophy governed their investment patterns. This is true for all investors. So, tell me. What is your philosophy of investment?' he probed.

'What do you mean?' Vikram asked.

'Where to invest is a question that should come up only after you can answer why you want to invest, and after having set realistic investment goals. Do you want to allow your money to grow, and to help achieve one or a set of objectives, or do you want to get rich quickly or do you want to emerge as a champion performer in the investment market?' demanded Rohan.

Vikram was listening intently.

*What is **YOUR** philosophy of investment?'*

'Moreover, you need an investment philosophy to keep emotions in check. As has been pointed out by many experienced players in the market, emotion is an enemy when it comes to investing. A 2018 study published in the Journal of Financial Planning found that investors, who used a behaviour modified approach to investing, that removed emotion, saw returns up to 23 per cent higher over 10 years. With more and more adults responsible for their own retirement planning, self-managed investing has become a critical life skill. That means we need to learn how to manage our financial emotions if we ever hope to retire,' Rohan advised.

'Let me share an example. The best buying opportunity in recent memory in the US was the March lows of 2009. That trough offered investors an incredible opportunity to buy shares of large household names for pennies on the dollar. Companies like Bank of America, General Electric, and Wells Fargo were all trading in single digits. Many of these companies went on to grow 500 per cent or more over the following years. Yet, fear pushed many middle class workers out of stocks entirely. Nearly two-third (63 per cent) Americans owned stocks in some form in the mid-2000s, according to a 2019 Gallup poll. After the global financial crisis, that number dropped to roughly half. Those who shied away from stocks missed out on the longest bull market in history, from 2009 to 2020. They let their fear get in the way of building wealth,' he noted.

'This is critical because most small investors get trapped in the speculation net as they lack a clear objective. Let me tell you a story which has now become folklore. It has valuable lessons,' he asserted.

A troop of monkeys lived near a village. One day, a merchant came there to buy them. He announced that he would buy each monkey at Rs 100. The villagers thought that the merchant was crazy. They wondered how somebody could buy stray monkeys at such a high price. Nevertheless, a few monkeys were caught and sold to the merchant, who paid Rs 100 per monkey, as he had announced. This news spread like wildfire. People started catching monkeys and bringing them to the merchant. After a few days, he declared that he would be buying monkeys at double the price. Even lazy villagers sprang into action at this and scampered about to catch the remaining monkeys. They sold them at Rs 200 each. Then, the merchant announced that he would be buying monkeys at Rs 500 each! The villagers were completely flummoxed. They caught the remaining half a dozen monkeys, and got paid Rs 500 each. The villagers began waiting anxiously for the next grand announcement. But the merchant informed them that he was going home for a week. He assured the puzzled villagers that when he returned, he would buy monkeys at Rs 1,000 each.

He asked his employee to take care of the monkeys he had bought.

The employee was alone and had to take care of all the monkeys in a cage. The villagers were sad as there were no more monkeys left for them to sell at Rs 1,000 each. The wily employee then told them that he would sell some monkeys to them at Rs 700 each. Very secretly, of course.

Reasons for not investing in the last 20 years

2000	Technology correction
2001	Recession, World Trade Centre attack
2002	Corporate accounting scandals
2003	War in Iraq
2004	Massive trade & budget deficits of the US
2005	Record oil & gas prices
2006	Housing bubble bursts
2007	Subprime mortgage crisis
2008	Banking & credit crisis
2009	Recession, credit crunch
2010	Sovereign debt crisis
2011	Eurozone crisis
2012	US fiscal cliff
2013	Federal Reserve to taper stimulus
2014	Oil prices plunge
2015	Chinese stock market sell-off
2016	Brexit, US presidential elections
2017	Stocks at record high, bitcoin mania
2018	Trade wars, rising interest rates
2019	India GDP at 5%
2020	Covid-19

As the news spread, the villagers started flocking to the employee. Since the merchant had promised to buy each monkey at Rs 1,000 each, there would still be a profit of Rs 300 on each monkey. The next day, the villagers queued up in front of the monkey cages. The employee sold all the monkeys at Rs 700 each. The rich bought monkeys in large lots. The poor borrowed money from money lenders and also bought monkeys. The villagers took care of their monkeys and waited for the merchant to return. But nobody came. So, they approached the employee rather anxiously. But he, too, had mysteriously vanished. That is when the villagers realised that they had been fooled into buying the worthless, stray monkeys at Rs 700 each.

'Once you have decided the goal of investing, formulating a plan and sticking to it constitutes the basic discipline of stock market participation,' noted Rohan. 'Of course, you can get lucky and hit the jackpot once in a lifetime. Maybe twice. But it would be erroneous to start banking upon Lady Luck and thereby running blindfolded, and taking

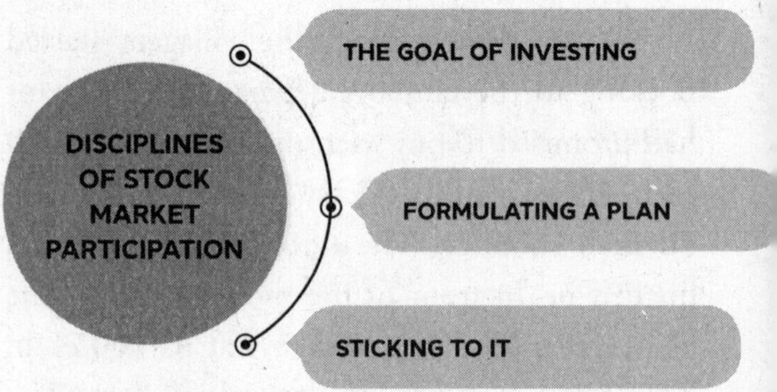

aimless risks. You don't know where such an approach will lead you,' he warned.

'That is precisely why you need to identify your mindset and fine-tune it to yield results in the stock market. "Gnothi Seauton" – the Greek maxim inscribed on the temple of Apollo at Delphi, or "Atmanam Viddhi," as instructed by our Upanishads is as much applicable to the stock market investor, as it is to the realm of metaphysics, or other fields of our mundane lives. Both mean "know thyself",' Rohan explained.

'Look, Rohan. I understand that setting goals for returns on investment depends on a number of criteria, most important of which includes age and current financial situation.

Ideally, of course, one should start investing at a young age, as soon as one starts earning. I know I missed the bus then, but you will agree that the ideal in the real world is more of an exception than the rule,' Vikram offered his point of view. He added, 'From whatever little experience I have had, I've learned that investment goals in the real world often become moving targets, with plans running into unforeseen roadblocks that force a detour.'

'That is quite true, Vikram, but please listen to me when I reiterate the importance of discipline in investing. It is absolutely essential to find success, to be successful,' Rohan argued. 'An investment plan requires one to acknowledge that one must sacrifice instant gratification for a larger goal, one must balance budgets, and one must fully appreciate that disruptions have a direct impact on the wealth and lifestyle goals. This necessitates setting a priority list of everything one truly values in life,' insisted Rohan.

'Yes, I am aware of these. It is also advisable to categorise investment goals into short, intermediate and long term segments, if possible, assigning clear timelines to monitor and track growth. For instance, buying a car in the next two to three years can be termed a short term goal. Accumulating funds to contribute to a corpus to buy a house in five to seven years is a mid-term goal. And, retirement plans or higher education plans for the children is a long term goal, if one starts investing early. My investment manager told me about these basics,' Vikram explained.

What are YOUR short, intermediate and long term investment goals?

SHORT	INTERMEDIATE	LONG

'Correct. Your age, financial situation and goals will also determine your level of risk tolerance. Are you the sort of investor who is ready to accept the upside as well as the downside of taking risks? More risk means higher returns, while lower risk means the gains won't come quick but that they will be slow and steady. The flip side of high risk investments is that there's a greater possibility of losses. Theoretically speaking, the younger you start investing, the more appetite for risk you can afford. It is, therefore, crucial to be sure of whether you are risk averse or whether you are ready to take calculated risks even if that means potential losses,' elaborated Rohan.

'However, these questions address only the components of investment strategy. Investment philosophy is something broader,' he added, and bent forward, closer to Vikram, to stress his point forcefully.

'Some time back, I came across a telling description of investment philosophy by Aswath Damodaran, Professor of Finance at the Stern School of Business at New

York University. He described investment philosophy as "a coherent way of thinking about markets, how they work (and sometimes how they do not operate), and the types of mistakes that you believe consistently underlie investor behaviour". Investment strategies flow out of investment philosophy, and one can go back to these sets of core beliefs in order to generate new strategies when old ones do not work,' he advised.

'That is an interesting way of thinking,' accepted Vikram. His interest was stoked.

'Ordinary investors rarely give enough thought to it, but the absence of an investment philosophy can cost one dearly, according to Damodaran,' Rohan said. Adding: 'The core set of beliefs acts like a rudder for an investor. Without this, one can easily fall prey to misleading claims of magic strategies, and switch strategies, resulting in high transaction costs, or even end up with investment strategies that are not appropriate,' he cautioned.

'What are the components of investment philosophy?' asked Vikram.

'There can be a number of parameters that constitute an investment philosophy, but some of the key components include investment duration (how long to stay invested), market timing (buying or selling financial assets by trying to predict future stock price movements), and asset selection (selecting the right assets based on past patterns or publicly available information—technical analysis or fundamental analysis),' responded Rohan.

The key components of **investment** philosophy

'That is a lot of information to process, I must confess,' Vikram said, shaking his head.

'Yes, as an investor, you will need to figure out your own philosophy of investment with the help of several methodologies that have been developed over many decades to understand stock market movements. It is important to study the movement of the stock markets—how they behave and how stocks perform with the help of all the research that exists. It is also crucial to stay abreast of developments in the economic and policy environment in which companies operate, as well as their internal functioning. In other words, a good investment philosophy must be well informed. There is no short cut,' warned Rohan.

'But if I remember correctly, you had advised that one must not be swayed by technical information or by jargon,' countered Vikram, a bit confused.

'Yes, you are right. I had clearly said that getting restricted by technicalities, much of which requires specialisation, can be counterproductive. It narrows down your perspective. But that is not in conflict with being informed, which is essential to broaden your horizon. And, that doesn't need any specialised, technical expertise,' Rohan explained. His advice seemed contradictory.

'Finance experts will hand you many tools to evaluate companies. *Technical analysis* for analysing past statistical trends to predict the future; *Fundamental analysis* to measure a security's intrinsic value by analysing relevant economic and financial factors to understand whether a security is undervalued or overvalued; *Alpha* to understand how a stock has performed in comparison to a benchmark index; *Beta* to understand how volatile a stock's price has been in comparison to the market as a whole; *Price-Earnings ratio* as a predictor of future stock prices, and many more. While each of these tools is useful and is used to predict future price movements of securities, not even one can be said to be precise and unerring. Had that been so, there would be many more stock market billionaires in the world,' Rohan argued.

'So, what do you propose, given that situation?' asked Vikram.

'An American gentleman had famously compared the stock market to a man walking his dog. The dog has tremendous energy. It seems to be jumping all around, trying to go in different directions, sometimes stopping, sometimes running. Basically, it appears completely unpredictable. Yet, you know where it is headed, because you know where the owner of the dog is headed. It is the owner who will take the dog to its destination. The problem with small investors, as has been rightly said, is that they focus on the dog, not on the owner. Therefore, pay more attention to the owner (business) and less to the dog (markets),' he counselled.

Here comes the little secret which I had promised to share with you. It's a framework that I have put together, in which you have to work through a set of filters that focuses more on the fundamental principles of good business and sound management, megatrends at the cross section of society and economy, and helps avoid certain sectors. It reflects my own investment philosophy, which is not dependent on the nitty gritty of financial calculus,' Rohan announced, taking out a piece of paper from his shirt pocket and handing it to Vikram.

'Take a good, leisurely look at it when you are free,' he said. He had the air of a secret agent in his manner of speaking. 'Let us call these *eliminators*, which when used appropriately will shortlist the companies where you can and should invest. However, these filters do not work in isolation, but in combination. The idea is to select the companies that sieve through all the filters. Only that can make your shortlist robust. Only then will you know which company to invest in and which ones to avoid. Enough for tonight. Let's wind up,' he suggested.

As Rohan was getting into his car, he stopped, stepped back and said this to Vikram. 'Hey! I almost forgot to tell you. I've fixed an appointment for you with Professor Bhupal of IIM on Monday afternoon. He's an expert on innovation. But make sure you go through the eliminator framework properly before you meet him,' he advised.

Vikram stood on the road for a few minutes, completely dazed. Where did the topic of innovation come from? What did Rohan mean? As his car drew up, he got in, telling himself that tomorrow would probably be a better day to start afresh and make sense of what he had heard.

THE CHEF'S SECRET RECIPE

To pick your stock, apply the following filters to the companies you are looking at. Also apply them to select companies that you might otherwise have ignored.

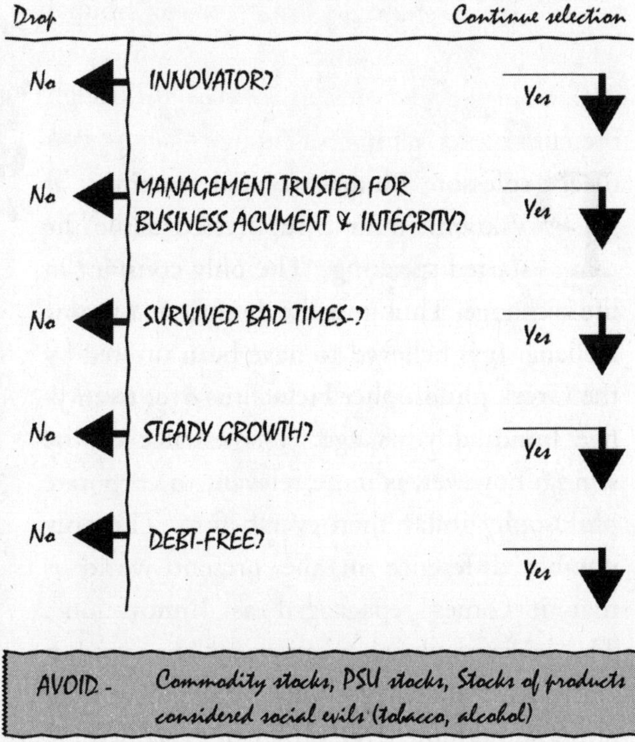

AVOID - *Commodity stocks, PSU stocks, Stocks of products considered social evils (tobacco, alcohol)*

Chapter 3

IN PURSUIT OF NEWNESS

Professor Bhupal looked intently at Vikram. With a suppressed smile, he started speaking. 'The only constant in life is change. Thus goes the dictum that is now a cliché. It is believed to have been uttered by the Greek philosopher Heraclitus over twenty-five hundred years ago. The essence of the saying, however, is more relevant to corporate philosophy today than ever before. The only notable difference in the present world is that it comes repackaged as "innovation". The lexicographical meaning of the word is "introduction of new things, ideas, or ways of doing something",' the professor explained.

'A few years ago, the Harvard Business Review published a letter from one of its readers, who captured the import of innovation, succinctly. "In a competitive market, value is constantly reshaped by innovation in an endless evolution towards perfection" he wrote,' said Professor Bhupal. He was trying to explain the importance of the first filter in the eliminator framework that Rohan had shared with Vikram.

Vikram had never thought that he would be sitting with one of the most well-known figures of management studies, getting exclusive time to understand the business implications of such a crucial subject.

Tall and imposing, Professor Bhupal, a specialist on innovation, was much sought after by corporate houses for his insights on current global trends. He was a non-executive director on the boards of six multinational companies and was on a few government advisory committees, as well. His columns in newspapers and business magazines were the topics of hot discussions on social media.

Vikram was not sure how, but the professor seemed to have known Rohan for a long time and he appeared to be very fond of him. As Vikram had walked into his office, the professor had welcomed him warmly. 'Welcome, young man! Rohan has been singing your praises,' he had said.

'A few years ago, Rohan and I had a very stimulating series of discussions on what parameters define the investment-worthiness of a company. Later, he shared with me the framework he had developed. I think it is a simple but brilliant piece of work,' the professor indicated.

'Do you really think so?' asked Vikram. He was surprised to know that Rohan had shared what he called his "Chef's secret recipe" with the professor, too.

'Yes, of course!' the professor retorted. 'You see, what that framework does is help you pick winners. It is a mechanism against over diversifying your investment portfolio,' he pointed out.

'But isn't diversification of portfolio an

investment basic, recommended by practically all investment advisors?' asked Vikram, slightly surprised.

'There are two ways to look at it. Diversification is recommended as a safeguard against losses, so that when some of your stocks go south, others might make up for it. Strictly speaking, it is not a growth strategy. Let me remind you what a famed billionaire investor said. He believed that diversification is required only when investors do not understand what they are doing,' revealed the professor.

'But that can be dangerous advice to follow, don't you think? To put all the eggs in one basket?' Vikram tried to comprehend the professor's logic.

'Well, for a casual, passive or uninformed investor, such a strategy can be dangerous. This advice shouldn't be taken lightly at all. It needs a lot of preparation on the part of the investor's behaviour, and above all, a nose for spotting trends. But if you study the eliminator framework carefully, you will see that it prepares you to make informed choices.

It compels you to study industry trends, and to keenly follow the reaction of specific sectors to market and regulatory developments. It prods you to understand the inner workings of companies,' the professor explained.

'No less important is the fact that a good portfolio can prosper for decades with minimal intervention. A basket of stocks is not a board game with turns and rounds. Rather, it should mostly be hands-off. After a proper allocation is set up, one of the biggest strengths of individual investors is what they don't do. They don't trade. They don't fiddle. They don't require daily monitoring. They let businesses earn profits and accrue to shareholders in uneven ways,' he continued.

'In a constantly changing world, a firm that produces new things is more likely to stay ahead of its competition as it will keep adding value to its existing products and services. This realisation is leading more and more companies to introduce newness in their offerings. In today's world of corporate catchwords, if sustainability has taken a central place, innovation is acknowledged as the driving force for growth,' he insisted.

What is your take on innovation being the driving force behind a company's business growth? Do you agree with Professor Bhupal's statement?

'Could you please elaborate, Professor? And, some illustrations should really help,' requested Vikram.

'Sure! Let me start with an example. When *maida* (refined flour) in instant noodles was flagged as a matter of health concern, Nestlé responded by launching an atta (whole wheat) noodles variant of Maggi. After the ban on Maggi noodles due to high levels of lead was lifted by the regulators towards the end of 2015, Nestlé put two new varieties on the shelves – atta and oats. More varieties like no onion, no garlic and Asian inspired noodles kept being added, responding to the extremely divergent food habits of the vast subcontinent. These products quickly helped Maggi recapture a dominant market share despite a five month ban,' noted the professor.

'So, the company was putting a whole new range of products to cater to consumer demand, and that's what drove up its market share?' probed Vikram.

'Absolutely!' replied Professor Bhupal, 'In other words, the company was consistently innovating. This constant innovation became the driving force behind its business growth,' he stressed.

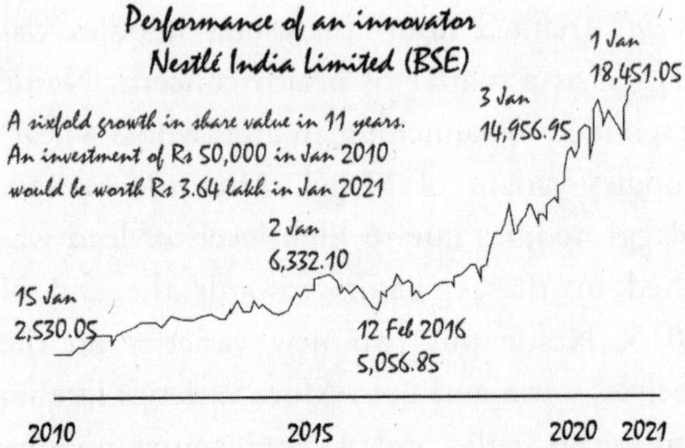

Source: Representative trend based on data sourced from Google Finance.

'If that is so obvious, why aren't all companies in pursuit of innovation? And, why isn't the same formula working for everyone?' thought Vikram. He articulated his question.

'You bet everyone is trying, but not everyone is succeeding,' responded the professor. He added, 'Just about any change is not going to bring in the growth. Changes can be incremental or radical, and products can be entirely newly designed. But to be successful, they have to add value to the customer, and they must stand out from the crowd,'

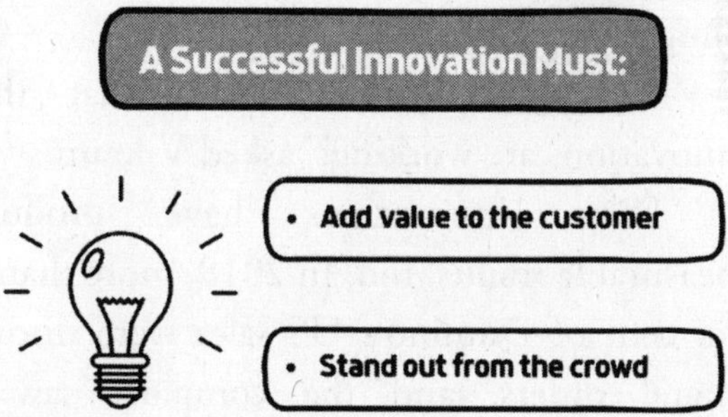

'Yes, that makes sense,' said Vikram, nodding. He was still mulling the idea. These insights were priceless.

'It is because the power of innovation is understood and appreciated that there is an explosion of the range in products from global brands like Domino's and McDonald's. They aim at capturing the favourite flavours of the local market: varieties of paneer pizzas, chicken tikka pizzas, aloo tikki burger, and paneer burger, among other things. Domino's is rated as one of the most innovative companies for a host of innovations starting with the thirty-minute delivery guarantee, online order tracking system, deploying cars with ovens, and delivering to outdoor locations,' Professor Bhupal elaborated.

'But how do we ensure that these innovations are working?' asked Vikram.

'These innovations have produced measurable results, too. In 2018, more than 60 per cent of Domino's US sales were through digital orders, and the company saw its stock rise 22 per cent in a turbulent market,' informed the professor.

'Some companies are extremely bullish on innovation. When 3M, the diversified technology company, best known for its products such as Scotch-Brite and Post-it, was ranked one of the world's most innovative companies for introducing roofing granules used in asphalt shingles to reduce smog, the company responded that it was just one of more than 60,000 innovative 3M products used in homes, businesses, schools, hospitals and other industries. One "can't think about 3M without thinking about innovation, which is at the centre of everything we do" asserted the company's CEO Mike Roman. One of the strongest points that the company has underscored is that it innovates across industry sectors: consumer goods, chemicals, and manufacturing,' remarked the professor.

'Reams have been filled up with research and information on innovation, and I do not want to lecture you on the technicalities. I only want to explain why I am going to use it as one of the filters,' the professor offered.

'You asked whether all companies are in pursuit of innovation. A case in point is Tiffany & Co., the New York-based luxury jewellery

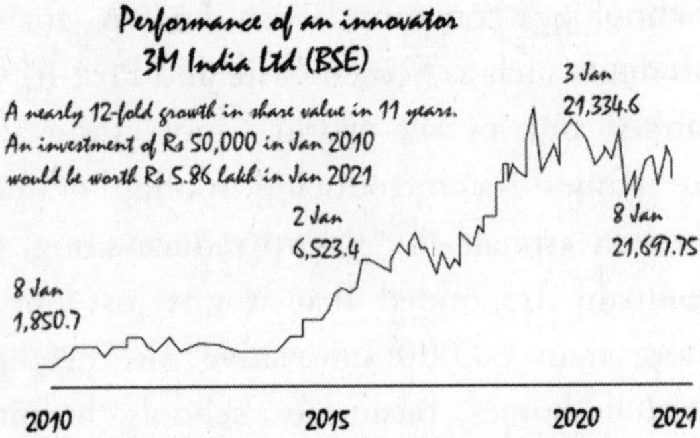

Source: Representative trend based on data sourced from Google Finance.

company, which started business in 1837. Soon after Frederic Cumenal became the chief executive officer (CEO) of Tiffany in 2015, he created a position for a chief sustainability officer (CSO), and planned a New York based innovation centre. One of the aims of the innovation initiative, he outlined, was to create new designs for changing demographics, especially new relationships such as same sex marriages, non-committal relationships, a decline in marriage rates in certain geographies, and evolving engagement rituals in other parts. The brief point I am trying to make here is that even the most well-known brands in the world have to be on their heels in order to respond to changing societal patterns and demands with new products and services,' he asserted.

'I see your point, Professor,' Vikram interjected. 'But my question remains as to how many of them succeed and why so many fail to take off? I am trying to understand this more granularly so that the catchword "innovation" does not become a blind alley in my investment decision making,' he maintained.

'That's a fair question,' conceded the professor. 'Innovation does not always mean growth in value. There are many cases where innovations have produced negative results. This happens because innovation is not a straightforward matter. It is a complex phenomenon situated at the cross section of firm level initiative and the operating environment, especially user needs. Often, simply producing new things does not suffice,' he agreed.

'Could you give me an example?' requested Vikram.

'Take for instance a study conducted by a team led by Paolo Aversa, professor at the

City University of London. This documented innovation in more than 300 F1 cars for over thirty years and matched their results in the F1 races. They found that in certain situations, more innovation led to poorer performance,' the professor recounted.

He added: 'There's more. The curious case of Royal Philips, the most valuable brand of Netherlands that has been a leader in innovation. However, in the first decade of the new millennium, the company's revenue declined by 40 per cent, profits were decimated and market capitalisation took a huge hit. The reason for this dismal performance was traced to excessive innovation by the firm. This uncontrolled proliferation of new products, often as standalone systems in different geographies and product lines, increased business complexities in the supply chain, and in sales and marketing, and in the administrative processes, as well. The direct impact was increased expenditure and customer and employee difficulties.'

What should a company's response be in

such a situation? Vikram wondered.

'The response shouldn't be to stop innovation. Instead, adequate care should be taken to formulate the right strategies to ensure their success. The researchers who studied the case of Royal Philips recommended a three-pronged approach. This included focusing on product integration for better performance, removing the barrier between innovators and the resultant complexity handlers (customer service, and operations, among other things), and creating a vision to help innovate for a purpose, and not just for the sake of innovation. As rightly pointed out by a Boston Consulting Group (BCG) report, continued success in innovation needs a well-tuned system,' averred Professor Bhupal.

Where does that leave us? Vikram thought to himself.

'The clear message that comes out of even failed cases of innovation is that, in the present world, a company cannot stop innovating. Failures will pop up now and then, but the bet still needs to remain on companies that

The 2020 edition of BCG's survey of top innovative companies records some interesting findings.

Firstly, keeping up with consistent innovation is not an easy job. Of the 162 companies that featured in BCG's top 50 most innovative companies since 2005,

- only eight have made it to the list every year;
- more than half appeared only thrice or less, and
- nearly 30% appeared just once.

Secondly, although innovation has become a buzzword,

- only 45% of the companies surveyed (among a sample of over a thousand most innovative companies), that is, less than half, have innovation as a top priority.
- 30% see innovation neither as a strategic priority nor as a target of investment.
- The remaining 25% are in a dilemma, with their investment not matching up with their stated priority for innovation.

endeavour to bring new things to the table. It is for the scholar to study and determine when and how innovations have worked and to get a grip on the dynamics of their success. For a lay investor, the criterion to keep in sight at all times is whether a company is investing to create new capabilities, and whether it is innovating,' he opined.

'All this is fine, but let me rephrase my question. Does the innovative capability of a firm translate into good stock market performance?' Vikram urged. He wanted to pin the professor down on specifics.

'To be honest, the answer is not unambiguous. And, that is because stock market performance is so complex that creators of highly complex econometric models, and even Nobel prize winning economists get befuddled by it. Yet, there are categorical views, such as that of Steven Vanelli, managing director of the US based investment management firm GaveKal Capital. According to Vanelli, companies that consistently employ innovation strategy exceed investors' expectations, which is reflected in the stock price,' the professor expressed.

'As an investor, one needs to look at the broad picture, and not get trumped by statistical modelling. I would like to reiterate that we need to rely on rational measures and those that make common sense. What therefore is perhaps most important in the BCG survey is that a greater proportion of companies which are committed to innovation (as reflected by actual investments) are ahead of those which are either non-committal or confused, in terms of rising share of sales from new products and services. What this means is that the companies which are serious about innovation are the ones racing ahead to put new products and services in the market. They find synergies in them and they are the ones reaping the benefits. That is reason enough to go with these companies,' he concluded.

Professor Bhupal stood up. He had to leave for a board meeting. 'I hope our discussion has helped you make up your mind, Vikram,' he checked.

'Of course, sir! Whatever you have shared

with me has been very useful and way beyond my expectations. It has cleared my thoughts and perceptions. I have much more clarity now,' Vikram admitted.

'I am glad. But my sincere advice would be – "Don't drop the ball here!" Follow this up with your own reading and analysis. Later this week, I am scheduled to have an interactive session on a different format of innovation. I'll be happy if you can attend that,' the professor said.

Vikram was only too happy to oblige. 'I wouldn't miss it for anything,' he confessed.

Later that evening, after the family had retired to bed, Vikram sat down with his laptop and opened his newspaper and magazine subscription portal. He needed to catch up with the latest developments. He realised that Rohan's and Dr Bhupal's inputs would be more useful if he weren't lagging behind when it came to the latest developments in the business world.

While surfing the journals, an interesting piece of information caught his eyes. It was a story on how Xiaomi, the Chinese multinational electronics company, founded in April 2010, had consolidated its position in India.

Xiaomi had flagged off its maiden flash sale for mobile phones on Flipkart on 22 July 2014. By the end of the year, it had launched power banks, and emerged as the fifth largest smartphone maker in India. In the same quarter the following year, Xiaomi sold one million handsets. A year later, the number doubled to two million. By the last quarter of 2017, the Chinese company had dethroned Samsung to become the market leader, a position it has since held on to. In an open letter, along with the IPO documents, Lei Jun, chairman and founder, underscored that Xiaomi is an internet company with smartphones and smart hardware connected by an IoT (internet of things) platform at its core.

In a subsequent meeting with Jun and board members, the question that was on top of everyone's mind was: What next? The brainstorming yielded a three pronged strategy. The first was to focus on consumer electronics and durables, including televisions, fridges, washing machines, air conditioners, water purifiers and laptops. This is a sector that can be a big revenue generator, but it is also extremely competitive. The strategy to beat competition was straightforward: to do something new that is disruptive of the existing market. The goal was attained by launching smart television sets. Within a quarter, Xiaomi became the biggest smart TV brand in India. In fact, it ended up selling a staggering two million units in just fourteen months since the launch. While older players like Samsung, LG and Sony were focusing on traditional TVs, and had priced their high end TVs prohibitively, Xiaomi had loaded its TV and sold it at half the price.

The second area that Xiaomi identified was small in business terms but growing rapidly. This included fitness bands, robot vacuum cleaners and air purifiers. The idea was simple: To own the category and develop it. In a short time, the company has come to account for more than forty per cent market share of this product category, growing almost twenty times in just two years. The third strategy had less to do with business and was more for the community of users built around the Mi brand—to keep them engaged and connected.

The company was smart enough to realise that smartphones alone couldn't assure it its top position. Xiaomi's transition to a smarter lifestyle brand is based on the understanding that it has to reach out to its users and stay connected with them through different products. Smartphones are the easiest way to understand the minds of the consumers. The idea for the company is to become the leading innovator in the technology space. Every six months, it launches a new product connected to the internet, to dominate any category that can be accessed wirelessly.

An agile organisation is constantly on the lookout to innovate, Vikram told himself. Dabur's case confirmed that.

Dabur found out that within a month of the Covid outbreak, "immunity" was among the most searched words online, reflecting the shift in consumer preference. The search for "immunity" and "Vitamin C" increased manifold in 2020. With heightened concern for health and wellness, and the reality of widespread financial hardship, consumers were rethinking every purchase.

The challenge before a company like Dabur was to seize the opportunity in a very short timeframe. With that goal in mind, Dabur transformed the organisation during Covid to not only become more aggressive in R and D expenditure, but to ensure that the innovations were targeted and marketed quickly. With this strategy, Dabur was able to roll out over forty new products in three months since the Covid outbreak.

Vikram saw that several companies had utilised the challenges presented by the lockdown due to the pandemic to leverage technology for minor innovations that would keep the businesses moving. For instance, Bajaj Allianz Life Insurance found that the scope for face to face interaction, which plays a key role in life insurance business, had suddenly been severely curtailed. So, it launched an app based platform in just two months. The platform, which made face to face interaction and completion of application formalities possible through screen sharing, took the number of customer engagements from practically zero to several hundred quickly.

Vikram recalled that sometime back, a colleague had touched upon an interesting topic during a knowledge workshop. When a brand becomes synonymous with an entire product category, you know you have a winner on your hands. Remember Xerox for photocopiers? Mobil for engine oil? In India's FMCG space, similar feats have been achieved by products like Moov, Krack and Itch Guard, which have come to define the product category, he had mentioned.

Vikram noted something fascinating. The creator of brands Moov, Krack and Itch Guard again disrupted the personal care market with another innovation, a few years ago. Darshan Patel started his own venture, Vini Cosmetics, in 2009, and launched a product after three years that redefined the market for deodorants. Patel spent these three years in market and consumer research to conceive his new idea.

Entering this market segment wasn't easy as the competition was fierce. But his survey based research threw up other insights. He focused on the common shortcoming perceived by consumers in all the brands: their biggest complaint was that the deodorant cans depleted fast. That complaint led Patel to develop his new product: a deodorant without gas. He made longevity the selling point of his product in a market where smell was the key differentiator, and he won. Starting in 2011, Fogg emerged as the market leader in the deodorant category by 2013 despite the struggle to convince customers that the bottles were smaller because there was no gas in them.

The product has taken Patel on the road of increasing profits but the question now is whether and for how long he can sustain this dominance. Here again, comes the question of serial innovation. Can Vini Cosmetics match the innovative prowess of Fogg to extend its winning streak to other market segments? And, how will it respond when copycat formulations start entering the market?

Something curious was happening in the consumer goods industry, Vikram noted. The agile, digital-savvy smaller companies were trumping the big guns, it appeared from a number of research reports. At the same time, smaller but targeted innovations seemed to be giving better returns than big budget overhauls. Between 2011 and 2016, 22 billion dollars in FMCG sales shifted from larger to smaller companies in North America alone, according to Boston Consulting Group. Why isn't the enormous resource advantage enjoyed by industry leaders, giving them the competitive edge, Vikram wondered.

Surprisingly, the research reports pointed to the fact that the larger brand owners were achieving no appreciable impact on sales and revenue through innovation, despite an annual R and D spending in excess of one billion dollars on an average. The marketing investments of leading firms, by contrast, have had a better correlation with sales results. The researchers put the innovation investments of these firms into two categories. The first is called 'Lorenzian', as an homage to mathematician Edward Lorenz, a pioneer of chaos theory. Lorenz's insight was that small things can set momentous events in motion, like the proverbial butterfly's wings triggering a tornado. They called the second approach 'Newtonian,' based on Isaac Newton's law that every action has an equal and opposite reaction. In simple terms, for big returns, invest hugely.

The researchers concluded that at least in the consumer goods sector, the straightforward Newtonian approach no longer applies. The corrective measure for these large companies with big investments, they suggested, is not to shrink their investments to a Lorenzian scale, but to find better ways to make the innovations work. These include opting for targeted innovation along with sharper focus on small bets and a

Which approach of innovation investments appeals to you? Lorenzian or Newtonian?

few big ones. For instance, Reckitt Benckiser's innovation that emphasises incremental tweaks to existing products is carefully chosen to make big headway with consumers. For example, adding a rinse agent, some salt and a protective ingredient for ceramic glaze to its dishwashing detergent called Finish, was a sure hit. The researchers pointed out that even watershed innovations such as the iPhone would not have been possible without a series of minor technical breakthroughs behind the scenes.

The Newtonian companies, the researchers suggested, could also maximise R and D returns by opting to purchase innovations from other organisations which are better suited for the job, thereby outsourcing the risky realm of research and development.

For example, Nestlé recently inked a deal for a six-month exclusive access to Swiss private label chocolate supplier Barry Callebaut's newly created ruby chocolate, marketed as the first new colour of natural chocolate since white was introduced eighty years ago. In early 2018, Nestlé launched a ruby chocolate KitKat bar in Japan and South Korea, just in time for Valentine's Day. Companies can alternatively opt for acquisitions instead of outsourcing, as when Unilever bought Dollar Shave Club, or PepsiCo purchased Soda Stream, a maker of home carbonated beverage devices.

Following his discussion with the professor, Vikram wanted to have a look at those examples where the giants of the day had faded away due to their failure to innovate. There were some big names here. Brands that had an air of invincibility. Names such as Blackberry, Kodak and Xerox that most of us are familiar with. Brands that were a part of our regular life and then someday made us wonder what happened to them. There are many other examples such as Yahoo, Nokia, Segway, Hitachi, and Toshiba. The story, clearly, is not always about failing to innovate, but about not being able to bring it to the market in order to grow business.

Following the same pattern, the top four Indian mobile phone handset players, too, have lost out their combined share of the smartphone market from over 23 per cent in the first quarter of 2014 to less than 3 per cent in the first quarter of 2019. Micromax, Intex, Lava and Karbonn, which made their way to the Tier II and smaller cities, lost the plot due to the lack of new products and their failure to adapt to the shift in technology. Companies like Xiaomi, Vivo and Oppo, which competed aggressively, with better products, eroded the market base of the former market leaders.

The Blackberry knockout

In 2007, when Steve Jobs announced the launch of the iPhone, a phone that could download music, videos and maps from the Internet, Mike Lazaridis, the CEO of Research in Motion (RIM)—then the world's largest smartphone manufacturer did not see it as a threat to the company's core offerings.

Mobile access to Internet content wasn't going to impact the BlackBerry phones' secure and efficient communication that was valued by its corporate customers.

RIM was not prepared for what happened next. They had been left behind by a phone whose battery lasted less than eight hours, operated on a slower second-generation network, wasn't secure and a keypad that wasn't as efficient.

When RIM did try to adapt in the face of the iPhone's massive success, BlackBerry couldn't execute properly. The launch of the touchscreen Storm in 2008 was a failure. The market share of Blackberry, which at its peak was 20% of the global smartphone market, crashed to 0.05% by the fourth quarter of 2016. BlackBerry's stock price, which was at a peak of USD 138.9 in May 2008 crashed to USD 6.7 in August 2012. BlackBerry announced in September of 2016 that it would stop manufacturing phones and instead focus on software.

Xerox: Failure to capitalise

"HOW CAN YOU ACCUSE ME OF TURNING MY BACK ON INNOVATION?"

The brand name of Xerox has almost been synonymous with photocopying, so much so that people used to ask for Xerox copies when they really meant photocopies. The instance of Xerox, however, is not its failure to innovate, but to capitalise on the business potential of its tremendous inventions.

In fact, the company set up the Palo Alto Research Centre (PARC) in 1970 that went on to develop the first personal computers, Bitmap displays, graphical user interfaces, word processors, computer mouse, ethernet, peer-to-peer and client server computing, and laser printing, among others.

Steve Jobs famously said that 'Xerox could have owned the entire computer industry.' Xerox failed to transform this innovation into profitable business models. Facing competitive disruption in the copier business from Japanese competitors like Canon and Ricoh, the laser printer became the engine of the company's growth. Yet, this growth was no match for the missed possibilities. Prices of the company's stock fell from a peak of USD 159.64 in January 1999, to USD 16.23 by February 2001. Since then, the stock price has not crossed the three-digit barrier.

The Kodak & Fuji story

The market leader in photographic films failed to innovate and lost out to the transition to digital photography. It is ironic that the world's first consumer digital camera was developed by a Kodak engineer in 1975, but the management refused approval to launch it commercially.

At its height, Kodak's market share of the photographic film market was more than 80% in the US and about 50% globally. The company filed for bankruptcy in 2012.

A study in contrast is Fujifilm, Kodak's chief competitor in the photo films market. While Kodak saw a 48% decline in sales between 2000 and 2010, Fujifilm succeeded in increasing it by 57%, by innovating. Leveraging its photo film technologies, the company created a variety of high-performance films essential for making LCD panels for TV, computers, and smartphones. It also diversified into entirely new markets such as cosmetics and drugs.

Other big companies that failed to innovate

Nokia
Blockbuster
Yahoo
America Online
IBM
General Motors
MySpace
Commodore Corp
Hitachi
Polaroid
Toshiba
Motorola
Palm
Sony
Pan-Am
Netscape
Compaq
HMV

Demand

[di-'mand]

An economic principle referring to a consumer's desire to purchase goods and services and willingness to pay a price for a specific good or service.

Investopedia

Chapter 4

CREATING NEW DEMAND

When Vikram walked into the seminar room, Professor Bhupal had already started speaking. He was referring to types of innovation as categorised by a paper published in the *Harvard Business Review* in May 2012.

Vikram moved closer to the podium and took a vacant seat. The audience consisted of students of management institutes, a few professors and some young professionals. There will be a lot of questions, Vikram thought to himself with a smile.

'Companies can choose core or incremental innovation, adjacent innovation, which is extending products or services to a new space, or transformational innovation, which is not only about new products and services, but about creating demands for products and services that didn't even exist. Most companies are heavily oriented toward core innovation because of the high risks involved in adjacent and transformational initiatives. Yet, the transformational initiatives are really the engines of blockbuster growth. Let us spend some time here to understand these companies in a little more depth,' began the professor.

'Marketing gurus will tell you about the different types of demands, ranging from a negative, bleak scenario (where a market is unreceptive) to the best case scenario of full demand (when the level of demand in a market is just optimal for an organisation). There are other types of demands such as falling demand and irregular demand, but I would like to focus today on "latent demand" and "no demand",' he said.

'Latent demand represents a consumer need that cannot be satisfied by any existing product or service, and the "no demand" scenario is one where it becomes essential to create a demand for a product or service. The distinction between these categories can often be fuzzy, making it difficult to position real world examples into neat exclusive categories,' he explained.

'Any discussion regarding transformational innovation tends to hover around technology, and with good reason. Take for instance, cloud computing. It is an idea that has been around since the 1960s but was applied commercially,

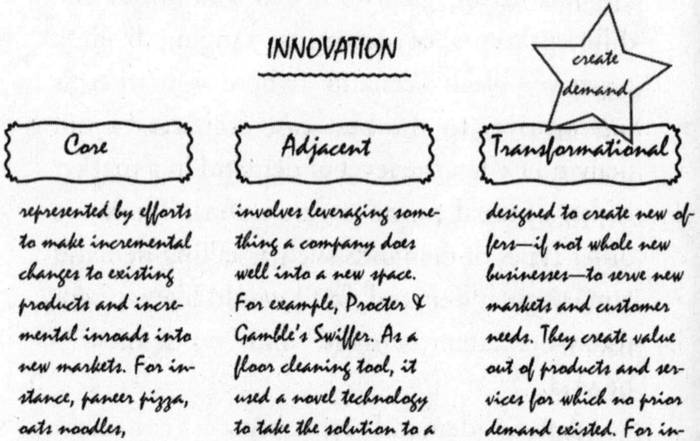

Source: Harvard Business Review, May 2012.

at a large scale, only in the latter part of the first decade of the new millennium when companies like Google, Amazon, Microsoft and IBM started offering software products and services that would not be hosted in hard drives of computers but on the Internet,' he pointed out.

'Or, consider artificial intelligence. With the explosion of digital data, companies are now adapting to this new and evolving technology to serve customers better, to make their own processes more efficient, to treat patients and for a host of other functions. Surely, even our parents never imagined, when they had to physically visit a bank, that in the new millennium all they would need to do is open a website, and be helped by a chatbot. Or, that they would have a small device in one corner of a room which would interact with them like a human being, switching on lights, placing orders for groceries, calling a taxi and even answering general knowledge questions,' he went on.

'These technologies are now rapidly

transforming businesses across the world. Although the start has been slow in India, companies have picked up pace and are rapidly adopting new technologies to offer new services. A 2019 NASSCOM report estimated that cloud spending in India in 2018 was around 2.5 bn US dollars, representing 6 per cent share of relevant IT spending, compared to 7.9 per cent share globally and 11.4 per cent in the advanced countries. Indian companies are, however, slated for a faster rate of growth in spending on cloud technology in the near future. While the global spending on cloud technology is projected to increase at 16.5 per cent up to 2022, the growth rate for India is expected to be nearly double, at 30 per cent. A May 2019 report by Microsoft and the International Data Corporation (IDC) predicted that by 2021, artificial intelligence will double the rate of innovation and employee productivity,' he pointed out.

'Professor, could you kindly give an example from India?' a student asked.

'Of course!' retorted Professor Bhupal. 'As

far as India is concerned, a product that created a niche for itself over three decades ago, and continues to dominate the market is not a high tech one. In a country famous for its diverse and complex culinary habits, the success of Maggi instant noodles in India is a wonder. Introduced in 1983, when the country was still short of globalisation, the brand established itself quickly by creating a need which was barely there: the need for a food item that wasn't regular fast food, which could be home cooked and which could be ready in just two minutes. Maggi noodles have had many imitators but none has been able to dislodge it yet. Since its launch, the brand has expanded to not only different flavours of instant noodles, but to ketchups, sauces, soups, spice mix, instant pasta and traditional Indian breakfast items like Poha and Upma,' he expounded.

'You might want to ask how this reflects in Nestlé India's books? According to the company's own estimates, total shareholders' return increased 2,463 per cent between 2001 and 2019, with an annualised return rate of 19.5 per cent. Its market capitalisation increased 28.7 times during the same period, compared to the 12.2 times increase of the FMCG benchmark index,' he said. The professor paused briefly, and looked at the student who had asked the question.

He then continued: 'Think of an urban young adult's daily routine not too long ago, say, the year 2000, and compare it with 2020. After waking up in the morning, young adults brush their teeth, freshen up, have breakfast and then think of catching up with friends in college or going out to play a game. Who would have thought two decades ago that the first thing to do once we woke up would be to check Facebook, WhatsApp, Twitter, Instagram and emails on a handheld phone?'

'Let's look at Apple. When Apple launched the iPhone in 2007, the direction of evolution of the mobile phone was clear: a handheld phone that was to transcend calls and text messages, and become a computer. The progress, however, left much to be desired. According to the *Wall Street Journal*, most smart phones had lousy software, confusing user interfaces and clumsy music, video and photo playback. It was at this stage that Apple made a breakthrough. Reviewing the first iPhone in the WSJ, Walter S. Mossberg and Katherine Boehret described the new product as a beautiful and breakthrough handheld computer,' the professor remarked.

'Its software set a new standard for the smartphone industry. The finger touch interface dispensed with the stylus and buttons. It included voice calling. It built upon the iPod. It had the best web browser, and also a strong email software. Apple had catered to the latent demand among high value customers, which came at a premium. It became the first company to hand the market a product that henceforth defined the nature of demand. The product became a point of reference,' the professor pointed said.

'The company had done the same with the iPod. This was an instance of one transformational innovation being replaced by another. The first product that stormed the market was the Walkman, a compact playback device with a headphone, introduced by Sony in 1979. A new era of listening to music was introduced, and Sony held half the market share in the US and in Japan for the next decade despite competition that tried to catch up. By the late 1990s, however, digital music started replacing cassettes. Songs in the MP3 format were the new rage. MP3 players started making their presence felt worldwide,' he observed.

'As the portable music market was in a flux, Apple made its move. It announced the iPod in October 2001. It could store up to a thousand songs, which could be browsed and bought from the iTunes music store. It had an intuitive interface, and seamless management through the iTunes software. Over the years, more and more customers went for the newer and improved versions of the iPod. By 2008, the iPod was able to capture 48 per cent of the MP3 market share, with its closest competitor at just 8 per cent. The iPod transformed the way people listened to music. Curiously, however, it, too, began its decline with the introduction of another transformational innovation—the iPhone, which was presented to the world by Steve Jobs as a combination of three products: "a widescreen iPod with touch controls," a "revolutionary mobile phone" and "a breakthrough Internet communications device",' the professor said.

'Experienced car drivers from the previous generation are more likely to defend their driving abilities. They didn't need a screen in front of them mapping out the best way to reverse a car, or the best trajectory to park a car anywhere. They would be quite astonished to learn that they could talk to their cars now. They didn't need these facilities. But now, we do, because once they have been shown to us, our generation and the next ones have come to appreciate their

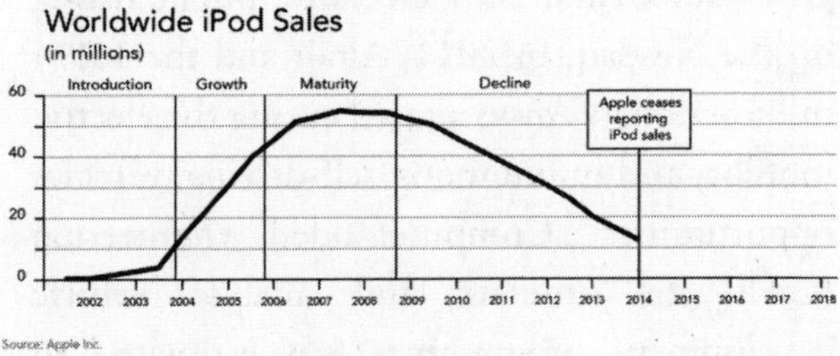

value. Information technology is revolutionising the traditional transportation industry, just as it is affecting other sectors,' he noted.

'Market analysts point out that Big Auto has globally moved its focus significantly from mechanical systems to electrical and electronic systems with software. The former has not diminished in size, but the role of software and electronics has overtaken the quantum of work on the mechanical side. With engineering R and D funds overwhelmingly behind software and electronics, it is growth time for niche software companies like Altair Engineering, Ansys and Dassault Systemes, even as other equipment manufacturers worry about their investments in internal combustion engine technologies. In November 2017, James Scapa, CEO, took Altair to a successful public listing on the Nasdaq. In 2011, Altair and the 1,294 million dollars Ansys started eyeing the electric mobility and autonomous (self-driving) vehicles opportunities. Computer-aided engineering (CAE) to simulate and analyse vehicle development programmes was estimated to have a market size of about 7.8 billion dollars in 2021. Altair acquired eleven companies in the run-up to its IPO in 2017, buying strategic IP assets, and approximately 200 developers with expertise in electronics, material science, crash and safety, industrial design and rendering. That's the kind of transformational push the conventional industries are adapting to. The future is changing rapidly,' he affirmed.

Creating demand where none existed. So, that's the other type of innovation the professor was referring to, Vikram thought to himself. He nodded in appreciation.

The talk was over. Dr Bhupal caught his eyes from a distance and smiled.

Having heard extensively about innovation, things were getting clearer to Vikram. He had already started thinking of the next filter that Rohan had listed in his note.

Chapter 5

VALUE OF INTEGRITY

'Let me tell you the story of someone who worked for two venture capital firms, before joining academia to research one particular aspect that she had noticed at those firms,' Jagdish Arora said, sipping his coffee.

He was a board member of the company for which Vikram worked. He was over from Mumbai for a board meeting, which had been suddenly cancelled. Vikram had been interacting with Arora for the past year, and had found him to be extremely knowledgeable about corporate governance. Arora was also a man of strict principles, which Vikram had occasionally experienced. With such a turn of events, and wisdom within arm's reach, Vikram took a shot. As it turned out, Arora was feeling chatty.

'The lady I am talking about routinely witnessed something in the VC firms that bewildered her,' Arora remarked. 'She saw that the VCs would get very excited on receiving and going through business plans from entrepreneurs, which would be followed up by research on the industry, leading to even more enthusiasm. But by the time the entrepreneur, on being invited, made his formal pitch in a meeting, they would have absolutely no interest in making an investment,' he pointed out.

'That's new!' reacted Vikram, rather intrigued. 'Why? What used to go so wrong?' he asked.

'Exactly!' said Arora. 'Why did a proposal that looked so promising on paper become a nonstarter when the person behind the plan actually pitched it? That is the question which the lady took up for her academic research. She worked closely with a California based network of angel investors. This is what she found,' he announced.

'Most entrepreneurs believe that the VCs' investment decision will be determined by the substance of their pitch. So, they prepare very well for that. But in practice, most VCs review pitch decks beforehand, and the interview with the entrepreneur is more about asking questions, gaining clarity, and sizing up personalities. Immediately after each interview, the investors fill out detailed questionnaires about their reactions and their views on whether to send the company through to the next step of due diligence, before taking the final call on investing. She found that interest in a company was driven less by judgments on the skill based competency of the founder, and more by perceptions about character and trustworthiness,' he elaborated.

'The thinking behind this practice is that a leader who lacks technical or financial skills can overcome that through training or by hiring the right talent. But character cannot be supplemented. And, this becomes a crucial factor, since angel investors and VCs often work closely for several years with entrepreneurs on risky ventures. They need to be absolutely convinced that their potential partners will behave in an honest and straightforward manner to set the right values for the management of the company. Her research found that the odds of receiving investment increased by ten per cent in the case of entrepreneurs who appeared trustworthy,' Arora pointed out.

That is fascinating! thought Vikram. He was truly impressed. He hadn't considered this angle before.

'Reputation pays dividends. Cut the clutter of management literature, and you will find the underlying message,' said someone. Vikram had been so absorbed in Arora's words that he hadn't noticed that Rohan had entered the room, and that he was standing behind him. He turned around, somewhat startled.

Both Arora and Rohan laughed at his reaction.

'Correct, Rohan. This is not mere theory. The reputation of a company's management is

Good Reputation of a Company acts as an Engine of Growth

not just a nice thing to have; it is absolutely essential. A company with a good reputation influences customer preferences, minimises competitive rivalry, increases its social status, and is allowed to charge higher prices for its products and services. In short, good reputation acts as an engine of growth. That's what investors look for. Think of the Tata Group, for instance,' Arora suggested.

'Researchers across the world have demonstrated that there is a strong relationship between a company's reputation and its performance even when the effect of other strategic variables such as product and market diversification, firm size, R and D, leverage and liquidity are removed,' reacted Rohan.

'You would already know about this, Mr Arora. Fortune's list of the world's most admired companies, a ranking of corporate reputation, conducted along with the global management consulting firm Korn Ferry since 1997, is considered the most authentic reference point for this purpose,' he stated.

'Yes, of course,' Arora replied.

'The nine parameters on the basis of which the rankings are done include a company's ability to attract and retain talented people, quality of management, social responsibility to the community and the environment, innovativeness, quality of products or services, wise use of corporate assets, financial soundness, long term investment value, and effectiveness in doing business globally,' noted Rohan.

'That is true, Rohan. But if you notice carefully, several attributes from among these nine actually flow out of just one: quality of management,' Arora pointed out. 'To put it in a more conversational phrase, one would term it the character of management. That's what determines how a company conducts its business, how it treats its employees, its attitude towards innovation, use of its assets, and the extent of vigilance towards its products, services and its financial state,' he elaborated.

> ***CORPORATE GOVERNANCE** is the system of rules, practices, and processes by which a firm is directed and controlled.*
>
> *Source: Investopedia*

'The metric that measures all this and more is called corporate governance. It encompasses everything that covers the company's business. Balancing the interests of stakeholders and of society, having adequate internal controls to ensure good business practices, and making sure that targets and objectives are consistently achieved. This contributes to not only maintaining the quality of a company's products and services, but to crafting its reputation for integrity and transparency. It helps companies avoid management level corruption, besides enhancing the firm's shareholder value creation and reducing investment and financial risks. It wouldn't be an exaggeration to say that good corporate governance, which in the final count, reflects the character of a firm's management, can make or mar its fortune,' he emphasised.

'A study based on the survey of more than 300 mostly C-suite executives and board directors conducted by Deloitte and Forbes Insights revealed that across industry sectors, reputation is considered the highest impact risk area to business strategy. Strikingly, the senior business managers and directors ranked risks to their firms' reputation above threats to their business model and the impact of economic trends and competition. Moreover, it is not a seasonal risk. As the then CFO of Marico told the Deloitte survey, "We don't see reputation risk management as having a start date and an end date". A company has to constantly be on tenterhooks about its reputation,' warned Rohan.

'I understand that the reputation of a firm or its governance standards can indirectly impact its bottom line, but is there any evidence that it also influences its stock prices?' probed Vikram.

Rohan's response was that studies from across the world have demonstrated that corporate governance practices have a significant influence on the stock prices of a firm. India is no exception. He elaborated: 'Analysing the results of the companies listed in BSE200, scholars from the Kumaon University found that corporate governance significantly affects the share price of these listed companies. Hence, it is a very important predictor for their share price value. That is, not only does the reputation for integrity and good business practices boost the current share prices of a company, but it holds out a promise for the future, too,' he opined.

'All this also translates to trust,' pointed out Arora. 'Do you trust a brand? Do you trust that the company can never do anything wrong? Do you trust that the company will never cheat you? As a rule of thumb, your money should be on the company that has your trust. In fact, the principle is so simple that it often evades our attention. Come to think of it: Would you invest in a company if you did not know whether you could trust it? You buy a bottle of Bisleri or Aquafina because you trust these names more than lesser known brands, although all of them might be selling the same product that meets the standards set by the country's regulatory authority. The same principle applies when you buy a laptop, or a car or a house,' he argued.

'This trust is monetised in the stock exchange. If you are an environment-conscious person, you will perhaps go for a Toyota. That's the image that has been painstakingly created by the company over a long period of time. A strong management ensures that a company's core values are not compromised,' he believed.

'To understand the value of that trust, one should look for cases where consumers have been let down, and their trust, broken,' suggested Rohan. In September 2015, one of the most trusted brands in the world shocked everyone. The United States Environmental Protection Agency (USEPA) announced that the German automaker Volkswagen Group deliberately tampered with the emissions control systems in its cars. With the help of a software, the company programmed the diesel

"The bad news is, our customers hate us. The good news is, we have a lot fewer customers than we used to!"

engines to activate their emissions controls only during laboratory testing to meet the US standards during regulatory checks, but emitted up to forty times more in the real world. In November, the company revealed that there were irregularities in carbon dioxide emissions and fuel consumption figures, too,' he said, giving out the details.

'The immediate impact was disastrous. Volkswagen had to recall about eleven million cars worldwide. Share prices tumbled by more than a third in the immediate aftermath. By 2017, the company estimated that nearly thirty billion US dollars had to be paid in costs, and the company's CEO and chairman were subsequently prosecuted. In 2018, thousands of shareholders and consumers took the company to court, seeking damages to the tune of ten billion US dollars. In 2019, the US Securities and Exchange Commission (SEC) sued the company on the charge of issuing bonds at lower interest rates than would have been possible had the company disclosed how polluting its cars actually were,' he went on.

'No less was the damage to the company's reputation. Brand Finance, a UK based brand valuation and strategy consultancy firm estimated that about ten billion dollars were wiped off Volkswagen's brand value, which was until then, the third most valuable automobile brand in the world after Toyota and BMW. That the automaker was even "willing to endanger its most valuable asset" through such cheat mechanisms astonished the CEO of Brand Finance,' he remarked.

Arora jumped up with a start. 'Oh my God! I am running late!' he said. He had just noticed the time. 'I must rush to the airport. But thank you, gentlemen, for a most spirited discussion,' he acknowledged before leaving hurriedly.

'I can see that you are making quite a lot of progress,' observed Rohan, with a smile. 'That's great! Keep it up! We will soon meet again to discuss some more points from my secret chef's recipe,' he assured Vikram and returned to his cabin.

Vikram was done for the day. He headed home. Reflecting on what Arora and Rohan had said, he decided to have another late night session to see what more he could pick up on governance and reputation.

It was already quite late by the time Sandhya took the kids to bed after dinner and a round of games. Vikram sat in the balcony and opened his laptop to surf magazines and journals.

The first article that caught his notice was about the findings of a team of top consultants from McKinsey that appeared to say the same thing about firms as about individual investors: that having a long term horizon was more beneficial. A company's management that works towards a long term goal is an asset that investors need to take into account while making their choice.

Vikram took a closer look. Studying 615 non-financial US companies from 2001 to 2014 (representing 60 to 65 per cent of total US market cap), McKinsey found that companies focused on the long term surpassed their peers, who were looking at the short term, on several important financial measures. They also created significantly more jobs. Moreover, these companies had delivered above average returns to shareholders, and had a fifty per cent greater likelihood of being in the top quartile or decile at the end of the period they measured. What if all American companies had taken a similarly long term approach? Extrapolating from the differences above, the team estimated that public equity markets could have added more than one trillion dollars in asset value, increasing total US market cap by about four per cent. And, companies could have created five million more jobs in the US, unlocking as much as one trillion dollars in additional GDP.

That made sense, Vikram thought. Having and adhering to a long term goal, instead of getting mired in the problem of ensuring immediate profit at any cost, did reflect the character of a company's management.

However, the report took one very critical view. Not every decision of a company should be for the long term. It is equally important to be agile and quick to respond to emerging situations regarding investment decisions. A shareholder must be alert to this agility of the management. That is another characteristic that defines the character of the management. The ability to judge and make quick decisions contributes to the progress towards the long term objectives. In fact, to win in the new era, successful managers don't behave as if every investment is a long term commitment. It is not necessary for them to predict the future accurately and know how a business will perform five or ten years down the line. Instead, they focus on whether putting money into something could be valuable as an experiment.

If the experiment goes wrong, they adjust. Treating investments as experiments frees companies to place more bets, and allows them to move faster than competitors, particularly in rapidly changing markets.

The report took Alphabet – the parent company of Google as an example. Since 2005, Alphabet has invested in countless new ventures. Some have been highly publicised, such as YouTube, Nest, Google Glass, Motorola phones, Google Fiber, and self-driving cars. Others are less known (grocery delivery, photo sharing, and an online car insurance comparison service). While many of Alphabet's investments have succeeded, a few have not. But rather than stick with those losers, CEO Larry Page and his team have shed them quickly. This has enabled the company to move on, test other investment ideas, and redouble its efforts in promising new businesses. In the past three years, Alphabet has closed the smart home company Revolv, shut down Google Compare (the car insurance site), "paused" Google Fiber, and sold Motorola Mobility to Lenovo. During the same period, the company has increased its stake in cloud services and various new undertakings managed by the company's X lab group, including electronic contact lenses and a network of stratospheric balloons intended to provide high speed cellular internet access in rural areas. Not every investment will pay off, but the "noble experiments" mindset has allowed the company to explore many innovative ideas and create new platforms for profitable growth.

Another sure shot sign of a company being run by a great management team is how they recruit, nurture and retain talent. There are many ways to increase output. All of them require talented people who can bring output-enhancing measures to life. In the new era, therefore, human capital—the time, talent, and energy of a company's people, along with the ideas they generate and execute—is the foundation of superior performance. A single great idea, after all, can put a company on top for many years. Think of Apple's iPhone, Continental Resources' introduction of horizontal drilling for oil and natural gas, and IKEA's reimagination of home goods. A lot of smaller, everyday good ideas can enable a company to pull away from competitors, too. But great ideas don't just materialise. They come from individuals and teams with the time to work productively, the skills to make a difference, and creativity and enthusiasm for their jobs. And above all, a company management that encourages its talent.

As long as companies continue to focus too much attention on managing financial capital, they will devote far too little to ensuring that the organisation's truly scarce resources—time, talent, and energy—are put to their best use. In fact, most companies lose nearly a quarter

FOUNDATION OF SUPERIOR PERFORMANCE

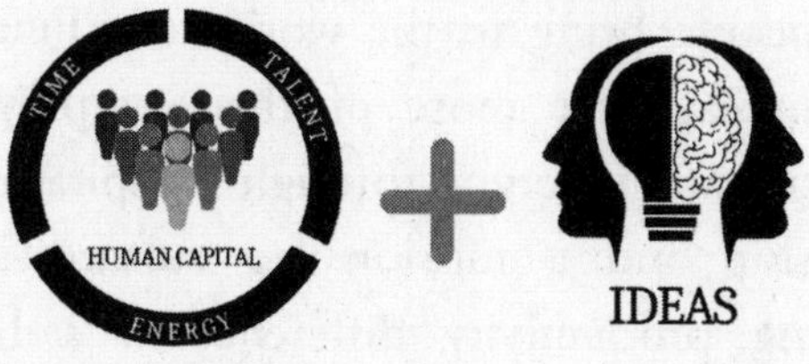

of their productive power because they have structures, processes, and practices that waste time and undermine performance. Firms counteract only a small portion of this lost output by making good hires and keeping their workforce engaged. In other words, human capital has become the fundamental source of competitive advantage, and companies that manage it as carefully and rigorously as financial capital perform far better than the rest. In their book *Time, Talent, Energy*, Michael Mankins and Eric Garton find that companies that apply real discipline in their management of human capital are on average forty per cent more productive than the rest.

These companies lose far less to organisational drag. They attract, deploy, and lead talent more effectively, taking full advantage of the unique skills and capabilities their people bring to the workplace. Finally, they unleash far more of their employees' discretionary energy through inspirational leadership and a mission led culture. The resulting productivity difference is a huge advantage for the best companies, producing operating margins that are thirty to fifty per cent higher than industry averages.

Now that's a parameter that's not too tough for an individual investor to follow, Vikram thought. But what really surprised him was the expansion of the idea of "character of the management". It appeared to be much wider in scope than he had originally imagined.

Another parameter that Vikram found aligned with the long term view of a management was that of purpose. Purpose, he realised, is an underrated attribute that is often overlooked while assessing the character of a firm's management.

Have you ever wondered about ***PURPOSE*** *while assessing the character of a firm's management?*

A group of researchers from top global business schools in Europe conducted a global study of high growth in companies, investigating the importance of three strategies known to drive it: creating new markets, serving broader stakeholder needs, and changing the rules of the game. The findings surprised them. Although each of those approaches did boost growth at the organisations studied, there was a fourth driver they hadn't considered at all: Purpose.

During the course of their study, the researchers talked to scores of C level executives, who had worked at twenty-eight companies in the United States, Europe and India that had had an average compound annual growth rate of thirty per cent or more in the last five years. What they learned from those conversations was that purpose played two important strategic roles. It helped companies redefine the playing field, and it allowed them to reshape the value proposition. And that, in turn, enabled them to overcome the challenges of slowing growth and declining profitability.

Low growth companies were found to spend most of their time fighting for market share on one playing field, which naturally restricts their growth potential. Due to fierce competition, gains in market share come at a high cost, often eroding profits and competitive advantage as offerings become commoditised. High growth companies, on the other hand, instead of being limited to their current playing field, think about whole ecosystems, where connected interests and relationships among multiple stakeholders create more opportunities. But these firms don't approach ecosystems haphazardly. They let purpose be their guide.

One company that has used purpose to redefine the playing field is the Finnish oil-refining firm Neste. For more than six decades Neste, founded in 1948, operated a business focused almost entirely on crude oil, but by 2009, it was struggling. The market was glutted, oil prices had dropped sharply, margins were falling, and the EU had passed new carbon emissions legislation. During the previous two years, the company's market value had shrunk by fifty per cent. Fighting those headwinds, the executive team, led by a new CEO realised that the company could no longer survive on its traditional playing field. It would have to look for new opportunities in the larger ecosystem. Renewable energy could be a key driver of growth, they realised. Their purpose, they decided, should be to develop sustainable sources of energy that would help reduce emissions, and everything they did would be guided by a simple idea: "Creating responsible choices every day". The new CEO launched a bold transformation, which the employees, customers, and investors initially resisted, but gradually accepted. The company made major investments in infrastructure, innovated renewable technologies, and engineered a fundamental change in its culture. All of this, put together, brought the company into a steep growth path.

There are three main ways, according to the researchers, that companies can reshape their value proposition. By responding to trends, by building on trust, and by focusing on pain points. For instance, Sweden's Securitas AB, a security company with 370,000 employees, traditionally offered physical guarding services. In the early 2010s, however, its CEO at the time, realised that globalisation, urbanisation, and the increasingly networked business landscape were all changing the nature of risk. While labour was becoming more expensive, new technologies were becoming cheaper.

Hence, the company's leadership decided that Securitas instead of simply selling man-hours, had to explore new ways of using electronics to provide security. Far from being a threat to the existing business, this

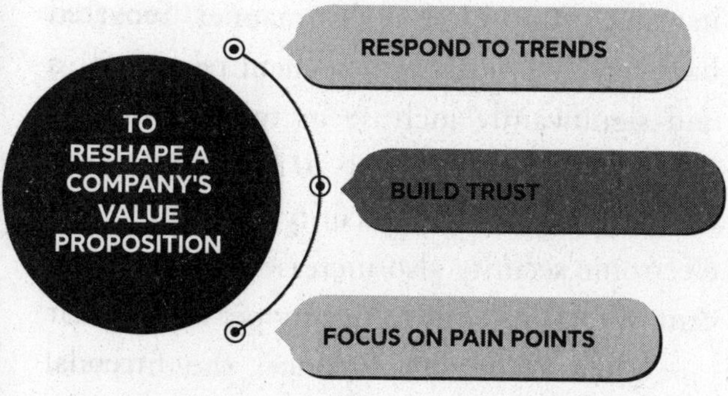

shift provided it with an opportunity to grow. In 2018, the company decided to go a step further, and reshape its value proposition from reactive to predictive security, a plan that once again built on the company's core purpose. The company, thereafter, strengthened its electronic security business by acquiring a number of companies, investing heavily in modernising and integrating back-office systems, and training its guards in remote surveillance, digital reporting, and efficient response.

That allowed Securitas to offer bundled, customised security solutions, encompassing physical guarding, electronic security, and risk management, allowing a much higher level of protection at an optimised cost. By expanding its value proposition in this manner, Securitas has been able to strengthen client relationships and significantly increase its margins for the solutions business. From 2012 to 2018, the company's sales of security solutions and electronic security also increased, from six per cent of total revenue to twenty per cent.

When Mahindra Finance, the financial

services arm of the Mahindra Group, wanted to define its value proposition, it looked to its parent company's long time purpose driven strategy of improving customers' lives, encapsulated in 2010 by the simple motto "Rise". In keeping with that strategy, Mahindra Finance decided to target its core offering, vehicle financing, to rural areas, where it could address the unmet needs of underserved customers in an underpenetrated market. That meant that the company had to figure out how to determine the creditworthiness of customers who were mostly poor, illiterate, and unbanked, with no identity documents, no collateral, and cash flows that were often impacted by monsoons. To do that, the company had to develop completely new ways to handle loan design, repayment terms, customer approval, branch locations, and disbursement and collection in cash. Not only that, it had to figure out how to recruit workers who could speak local dialects, assess local situations, and operate under a decentralized model of decision making. Remarkably, the company managed to do all those things, and it established a preliminary level of trust with its customers.

It then stretched its value proposition to help farmers and other customers obtain life, health and tractor insurance. In a country where insurance penetration is abysmally low (about three to five per cent), this was no small feat, especially since rural residents didn't easily part with any minuscule monthly surplus they had, even if it was to secure their livelihood. Then, Mahindra Finance extended its purpose driven efforts to housing finance, another arena in which it recognised that it could help its rural customers rise above their current level of difficulties.

Recognizing an opportunity, Mahindra Finance decided to play at the intermediate level, offering customised home loans at rates of about fourteen per cent, an option that appealed to its growing base of customers. When some of those customers developed successful small agribusinesses, they began looking for working capital loans, equipment loans, project finance, and so on. These were more unmet needs that

Mahindra Finance could address. So, it extended its value proposition again, into the small to medium enterprise arena, offering finance and asset management services. Throughout its expansion, Mahindra Finance was guided by its goal of helping rural citizens improve their lives. The company identified and committed itself to value propositions that allowed it to deepen its relationship with its customers, which in turn, created additional streams of revenue and profits. Today, Mahindra Finance is India's largest rural non-banking financial company, serving fifty per cent of its villages and six million customers.

Sometimes, one individual becomes the face of a company, which then follows the spirit imbued by the leader. This could be the company's founder or someone who joins later and transforms the company's image.

Saugata Gupta of Marico, for instance, has been recognised for his role in innovating to build new growth engines in skin care, male grooming products and health focussed packaged foods. He strengthened the structure Harsh Mariwala had created, by institutionalising Marico further, through stronger corporate governance, transparency and digital transformation. Marico is among a select group of Indian blue chip companies to have seen double digit revenue growth and return on capital employed each year since 2009. It enjoys a stable market share for its flagship products—Parachute coconut oil (53 per cent) and Saffola (73 per cent). Marico has since successfully transitioned from a family-run commoditised business to an institutionalised FMCG giant.

The company is evaluating a scenario where private supply chain logistics agencies carry out supplies, and distributors have zero stock. Gupta is one of the longest serving corporate heads at Marico and is looking to build a strong legacy, much like Mariwala did in the 2000s. A group of at least twenty young leaders is being groomed under Gupta. They are evaluated based on how they execute tasks; their learning ability and the way they nurture talent, appreciate shareholder value and imbibe the owners' mindset to their business. Marico today is a lot more institutionalised than some of its competitors. This is what makes it one of the more attractive FMCG companies for sales and marketing executives to work with in India apart from its work culture and empowerment opportunities. Marico now has outside coaches to train its staff and provide development tools to assess its young leaders. Gupta wants to continue pressing the innovation button, alter distribution schemes for new growth engines, and embrace digital technologies in marketing. In those terms, in just over a decade, he has already created his own legacy.

Similarly, Bhaskar Bhat helped transform Titan from just a watchmaker to the second most valued company in the Tata stable. Titan's journey started thirty-five years ago, in 1984, as a joint venture between the Tata Group and the Tamil Nadu Industrial Development Corporation. Bhat joined the company in 1983 in the marketing department of the Tata Watch Project. Since then, the company has evolved into a retail giant, branching into jewellery, eyewear, accessories, perfumes, tech wearables, and sarees. It was in 1994-95 that the idea of Tanishq was mooted, but it took time to hammer it out into a business model that could generate revenue. Today, Tanishq is Titan's flagship jewellery brand, with the entire jewellery segment, comprising the Zoya, Mia and CaratLane brands, and accounting for 84 per cent of the company's total revenue. Bhat has been involved in Titan's journey from the beginning and has helped it become a dominant player in the watch category, with 65 per cent market share. More than 80 percent of the company's revenue comes from the jewellery segment. But despite the success of Tanishq, Titan has continued to explore opportunities in other segments, such as watches. In this category, it has eight brands, from Fastrack, its most widely known, to Favre Leuba, the second oldest brand of Swiss watches, that it acquired in 2016. Recently, Titan also launched online sale of clocks.

Since he took over as MD, Bhat has ensured that there is a cultural change within Titan in terms of creating strong leaderships, and for building a culture of value that permeates through the entire ecosystem.

Similarly, Anil Rai Gupta, Chairman and MD propelled Havells India into its next phase of growth with a strong focus on research and development, manufacturing, and nurturing a culture of entrepreneurship. The group already has significant play in the Indian fast moving electrical goods and electrical equipment category. Havells manufactures everything from fans, water heaters and personal grooming products to cables, wires, air conditioners, washing machines and television sets. As India grapples with a slowdown, Havells has been focussing heavily on building up its manufacturing capacity, in addition to setting up a large rural network to piggyback on a revival in the Indian economy. The company currently has one of the largest market capitalisations in the segment.

The building blocks of a company's reputation was becoming clearer to Vikram. He now knew what to look for when applying this filter to choose companies in which he should invest.

Chapter 6

GOOD COMPANIES IN BAD TIMES

Resilience is a word which Vikram had often heard repeated in consulting lingo. One of his seniors had familiarised him with the famous quote of Reverend John H Moore, former Archbishop of Canterbury, who is believed to have said: "The real test in golf and in life is not in keeping out of the rough, but in getting out after we are in". However, he had never thought of it in the context of selecting stocks for investing. The chef's secret recipe now compelled him to think.

Vikram realised that the quote was remarkably apt for the corporate world. If the test for the character of a company's management is its way of doing business, a much more difficult test is how it handles a crisis. Every company goes through a rough patch, whether of its own creation or as a result of external factors. A company's mettle is proved by its determination, and the methods it applies to negotiate crises.

Vikram found one of the best examples of emerging stronger from a crisis in the story of Lego.

More than half a century after its founding, Lego "has consistently remained one step ahead of the innovation curve, releasing new products and finding new ways to engage users of all ages with its tiny, plastic bricks," wrote the *Washington Post.* Experimenting with new technologies, and perhaps more importantly, engaging its user base, has helped the company surge ahead in gaining new ground. The company's sales grew consistently for thirteen years (at double digits for a decade) until 2017, when it declined by 8 per cent. It quickly returned to the growth path in 2018 with a 3 per cent sales growth and a higher 6 per cent in

2019. The growth was all the more remarkable, as in 2019, the global toy industry shrank by 3 per cent.

From its founding in 1932 until 1998, Lego had never posted a loss, but by 2003, it was in big trouble. Sales were down 30 per cent year on year, and the company was 800 million dollars in debt. An internal report revealed it hadn't added anything of value to its portfolio for a decade. Consultants who hurried to Lego's Danish HQ advised diversification. The brick had been around since the 1950s. They said it was obsolete. Lego should look to Mattel, home to Fisher-Price, Barbie, Hot Wheels and Matchbox toys for ideas to diversify. In taking their advice, Lego almost went bust. It introduced jewellery for girls. There were Lego clothes. It opened theme parks that cost £125 million to build and lost £25 million in their first year. It built its own video games company from scratch and pushed forth the largest installation of Silicon Graphics supercomputers in northern Europe, despite having no experience in the field. Lego's toys still sold, particularly tie ins, like their Star Wars and Harry Potter-themed kits. But only if there was a movie out that year. Otherwise, they sat on shelves.

However, beating the threat to its very survival, in 2015, the privately owned, family controlled Lego Group overtook Ferrari to become the world's most powerful brand. It announced profits of £660 million, making it the number one toy company in Europe and Asia, and number three in North America, where sales topped 1 billion dollars for the first time. From 2008 to 2010, its profits quadrupled, outstripping Apple's.

Lego's revival has been called the greatest turnaround in corporate history. A book devoted to the subject, David Robertson's *Brick by Brick: How Lego Rewrote the Rules of Innovation*, has become a set business text. Sony, Adidas and Boeing are said to refer to it. Google now uses Lego bricks to help its employees innovate.

It was Vig Knudstorp, Lego's CEO, who turned around the company's fortunes by methodically rebuilding it, brick by brick. He dumped things that the company had no expertise in; slashed the inventory, halving the number of individual pieces Lego produces from 13,000 to 6,500, but increased the brick colours, and encouraged interaction with Lego's fans, something previously considered taboo.

The company used the internet creatively, allowing fans to share their creations. It promoted events like Lego fan conventions, and it launched its own crowdsourcing competition. Originators of winning ideas get 1 per cent of their product's net sales. What made the company successful again was its ability to create new entities, movies, and TV shows, by partnering with creative minds. It also started making hit toys again. Most impressively for a company with a customer base that in 2011 was 90 per cent boys, it finally cracked the girls' market. Lego Friends features a reconfigured "Mini doll" and centres on five characters in the fictional Heartlake City.

None of this has happened by chance. Lego

is said to conduct the largest ethnographic study of children in the world. "We call it camping with consumers" said Anne Flemmert Jensen, senior director of its Global Insights group. "My team spends all its time travelling around the world, talking to kids and their families and participating in their daily lives," she had revealed. Lego is increasingly concentrating on bridging the physical and the virtual. This year, it rolled out Lego Life, a social network for kids too young for Instagram, to share their creations, gaining 'likes' from peers and Lego characters alike.

Further impetus was provided by the Lego System of Play. Each new set not only brings twelve or so new possible models but it can also be combined with what a customer already has to lift the total number of potential structures by orders of magnitude.

This has a terrific network effect. If a child already has a Lego set, getting another Lego product is more valuable than just the incremental purchase. It extends the platform for play in an exponential way. And, it is infectious. The more one kid gets a Lego set, the more the other wants it, as well. Children who have Lego sets can also mix and match their collections.

Reading through examples and case studies, Vikram felt that typically, the companies that emerge successfully from difficult times are the ones which have an established tradition of not compromising with their commitment to integrity and stakeholder interests.

> **To emerge successful from difficult times,**
>
> **A Company must NOT compromise with:**

- Its Commitment to Integrity
- Stakeholder Interests

Nestlé, for instance.

"Beware! Eating 2-Minute Maggi Noodles can ruin your Nervous System" blared the headline of a news portal. The Food Safety and Drug Administration (FSDA) of Uttar Pradesh had found monosodium glutamate (despite a "no added MSG label" on packets of Maggi) and lead in samples of Maggi 2-Minute noodles. The quantities were much higher than permitted by India's food standards. Similar results were found in more samples in other states. The findings started a chain reaction.

Within days, the sale of Maggi was banned in Delhi, Assam, Gujarat, Tamil Nadu and Andhra Pradesh. The Food Safety and Standards Authority of India (FSSAI) ordered a recall of all approved variants of Maggi instant noodles and oats masala noodles. Maggi was declared "unsafe and injurious to health". The government claimed damages to the tune of Rs 640 crores from the company in a case filed in the national consumer court. Cases were filed against film stars Amitabh Bachchan, Madhuri Dixit and Preity Zinta, who had promoted the Maggi brand. The Central government followed with a nationwide ban for an indefinite period.

This was not only devastating for Nestlé's business in India, but it was a veritable nightmare for its brand image. How could a company that dominates the infant food and nutrition market be so careless about harmful chemicals in another food product that accounted for 63% of the instant noodles market in the country? Nestlé got some relief in mid-August when the Bombay High Court allowed it to resume the sale of Maggi on the condition that further tests by accredited laboratories found the levels of the chemicals below permissible limit.

'Maggi is the worst crisis that we have faced in the 104 years of our existence in this country; also the worst crisis the company has faced globally in a long time,' Nestlé's managing director told a business magazine later.

Maggi was relaunched after court mandated tests in November 2015, but in this brief period of a few months, the impact had been huge.

Nestlé had to withdraw all of its Maggi noodles from sale across the country—about 38,000 tonnes, and destroy them. It lost Rs 500 crore (77 mn US dollars) due to this crisis, which opened up the market to competitors like ITC's Yippee and Nissin's Top Ramen, and made space for the newcomer Patanjali with cheaper products. Nestlé's share prices dipped immediately but started an upward climb with the favourable court order. The company registered its first net loss that quarter in nearly three decades, returning to profits in the next quarter, but at a 60 per cent lower level when compared to the same quarter in the previous year. Brand Finance forecasted that the Maggi brand, which was valued at 2.4 bn US dollars prior to the crisis, and which made Nestlé the twenty-third most valuable food brand in the world, stood to lose over 200 mn dollars in brand value.

The prognosis was grim. The CEO of Brand Finance opined that Nestlé would have to turn around swiftly to ensure that the Maggi brand retained its dominance in the market. 'If not, the Nestlé brand itself could be at risk,' he had said. By all standards, the consequences of the ban were a serious threat to the business's growth, and the path to further decline was wide open.

If things were not already bad enough, Nestlé's lack of an efficient communication to its consumers, even when the matter had blown into a full fledged controversy, compounded the crisis. Its silence was interpreted as an admission that something was wrong. But the company stuck to its position that Maggi was absolutely safe for consumption and that it met all food standards. And, it continued to prove its point by extensive tests conducted on its products. The company pulled itself out of the crisis in a very short time, displaying the strength of its spirit. The managing director of Nestlé made it clear, once the favourable ruling from the Bombay High Court was delivered, that the company would focus on building the brand.

From its market share of 10.9 per cent at the time of relaunching in November 2015,

Maggi reclaimed the top spot (57 per cent) by June 2016. By 2019, Maggi surpassed the pre ban level of sales in terms of both value and volume.

Rebounding from a crisis without losing consumer trust is the litmus test of the character of a firm's management, Vikram reflected.

Soon after the emissions scandal hit Volkswagen, the US based analytics and advice firm Gallup conducted a survey to find out what consumers thought of Volkswagen in the wake of the scandal. Forty-one per cent of the respondents said that they were less likely to buy a Volkswagen model compared to 29 per cent, who said that the news had no impact on their consideration to buy one. Gallup also found that only 1.6 per cent of the respondents were aligned with the carmaker's desired brand description of reliable, fun and environmentally friendly, against 16 per cent who used words such as dishonest, liar and cheater to describe the company's brand.

Amidst this doom and gloom, however, there was a silver lining. The survey found that there was a core group of customers who strongly believed in the brand. Gallup suggested that Volkswagen's recovery would depend on rebuilding brand trust first with customers who were not fully engaged and then with new customers. Although the company publicly apologised and ran advertisements in major newspapers that it was going to "make things right," there was still a section of customers who felt that this was not enough.

In less than three years, Volkswagen's stock price was up ten per cent from the pre-crisis level, and the company outperformed its competitors

BMW and Daimler in sales. The company increased its profitability, and announced aggressive plans for new technologies: 25 bn Euros to be spent on electrification and 14 bn Euros on shared mobility and self-driving technology by 2025.

The company was still facing lawsuits and criminal probes, but it made a visible push for transformation strategic and technological. It chose to utilise the crisis as a catalyst for change rather than being pulled down by it. CEO Matthias Müller portrayed the crisis and its impact in a positive light. He described it as "a warning that things couldn't stay the way they were," and that "there was a need for radical change that would have previously been unthinkable or, at the very least, impossible to implement".

Vikram found another good example in the Indian ecommerce segment—that of Snapdeal.

A pioneer in the Indian ecommerce industry, Kunal Bahl co-founded Snapdeal—one of the country's earliest unicorns—in 2010, when he was just 24. Within six years, it became the second largest ecommerce company in the country, with a market valuation of 6.5 billion dollars. In that period, apart from becoming a darling among investors, Snapdeal boasted of some heavyweights as investors, including Ratan Tata, eBay, SoftBank and Nexus Venture. It also acquired eleven companies, the most notable being FreeCharge and Unicommerce. Then, in the summer of 2017, the dream run came to a screeching halt.

Seven years after it was founded, an imminent shutdown loomed over the Gurugram-headquartered company after a failed merger with Flipkart. It was left with inadequate funds, enough to barely last a month. Bahl and co-founder Rohit Bansal were in a similar situation sometime in 2013 when the funds had run dry, but 2017 was different. Raising money wasn't going to be easy and it would only mean the end of the road, as Amazon and Flipkart tightened their grip over the Indian market. Even the planned sale to Flipkart was at a fraction of its peak valuation of 6.5 billion dollars.

Now, in a span of three years, Bahl and Snapdeal are starting to script a turnaround. Over the last three years, Snapdeal has reduced its loss by an incredible 95 per cent, while revenue from operations has grown by 85 per cent. Traffic, the company claims, has seen a 100 per cent growth. Last year, more than 27 million unique buyers bought on the platform. And, amid the pandemic, it added another six million users and 20,000 new sellers, apart from its already existing 500,000 sellers.

'It is about focusing on very few things and doing those very well,' says Bahl. He believes it is a big learning for us as a company, as entrepreneurs, and as a management team that excellence comes with focus, and doing very few things really well. That focus on specialisation is what eventually brought Snapdeal to find a niche, and shift its attention to what it calls value ecommerce. The segment, Bahl claims, provides a 163 billion dollars opportunity in India, and involves selling unbranded or lesser known brands with very high value to the consumer, particularly in the low and middle income categories.

'It is about unlocking aspirations for those with less money,' says Bahl. According to him, "these customers are looking to make a discretionary purchase online but are fairly value sensitive. What they care more about is not for the big brand logo, but whether what they are buying is of value". With Jio entering the arena in 2016 and the 4G penetration growing quite dramatically, it brought millions of new internet users online. A large number of them belonged to the low to middle income demographic in the small towns of India, whereas earlier, it was mostly consumers from the big cities who were affluent and buying online. Further, they noticed that a lot of smaller, regional manufacturers and traders had started hopping online in the last four years. That meant taking a step back and devising a different tactic to the earlier version. According to Bahl, prior to 2016, it was mostly brands and branded products that were bought and sold online.

Although people aspire to buy expensive products, they lack the ability to do so. They do not, however, lack the aspiration to look and feel good. To tap that innate desire, Snapdeal began by building a portfolio of products that are not expensive or prohibitive because of their price. Potential buyers ought not to be dissuaded.

Bahl's plans got a much needed boost as India announced a lockdown in late March 2020, as the Covid-19 pandemic broke out. The lockdown meant a push towards ecommerce adoption, particularly for those who had remained sceptical about online purchases. Bahl reckons that the economic crisis that accompanied the lockdown also made customers extremely wary about their purchases. Snapdeal claims to have added six million new buyers during the pandemic.

Chapter 7

BET ON STEADY GROWTH

It was another weekend at Rohan's apartment. Vikram felt that he needed a sounding board to run all the ideas and the information that he had assimilated over the past month. Moreover, there were some more filters in the chef's secret recipe that he needed to understand.

'Can we meet both on Saturday and Sunday, boss?' Vikram asked. 'I really need your inputs,' he stressed.

'Okay, let's do it,' Rohan replied. 'But you will need to give me a cut from whatever money you make from the stock market after you have learned the secret recipe. I say 20 per cent,' he suggested, smiling softly.

Vikram laughed out aloud. Indeed, he had no words to express his gratitude to Rohan. His boss had been extraordinarily patient with him.

'One of our many weaknesses is the inability to apply the lessons that we learn in theory in real world situations,' Rohan said. It would be rare to find someone who isn't aware of Aesop's fable about the slow but steady tortoise and the fast but inconsistent hare. It often misses our attention that the lesson of the story is apt for the stock market, too. Especially when you are in the game for the long term.

'Remember our first round of discussions on investment philosophy?' Rohan asked. 'The biggest obstacle to wealth generation in the stock market is to give in to the greed of becoming super rich quickly. The temptation to go for stocks that surge in good times is too great for many retail investors. A few might even make significant gains if they are lucky. But the dice doesn't roll on command. The flip side is that if Lady Luck hasn't taken a shine to you, the chances that you will end up on the

VOLATILITY is a statistical measure of the dispersion of returns for a given security or market index. In most cases, the higher the volatility, the riskier the security.

Source: Investopedia

losing side are much higher. Hence, the need for caution and discretion,' he elaborated.

'I did some groundwork,' said Vikram. 'Stocks whose performance is inconsistent are called volatile. They can surge as quickly as they can fall. Hence, the potential to make quick gains goes hand in hand with the risk of losing money. Analysts use something called beta (β) coefficient as the metric for measuring the volatility of a stock in relation to the market. It measures how an individual stock moves when the overall stock market increases or decreases. The market movement is taken as the point of reference with a beta value of 1. If a stock swings more than the overall market over a period of time, it has a value greater than one (that is, relatively more volatile) and the stock that moves less has a value of lower than 1. By implication, it tells you that when the market moves upwards, your returns from the stock will be higher than the market average. But it also means that when the market goes down, you stand to lose more. In other words, such stocks have the potential for higher returns, but also higher risk. Conversely, the theory goes that stocks that have lower risks also give lower returns,' he expounded.

'What should you settle for then?' asked Rohan. Vikram was not prepared for this. As he fumbled, Rohan continued, 'Before we answer this question, let us look at an alternative theory.'

'There is a hypothesis called the low volatility anomaly or low beta anomaly theory, which directly contradicts the high risk, high return model. It claims that stocks with lower volatility have historically performed better than higher volatility stocks in the long run. It is, however, more than a hypothesis; it is now a proper theory, backed by data, and promoted

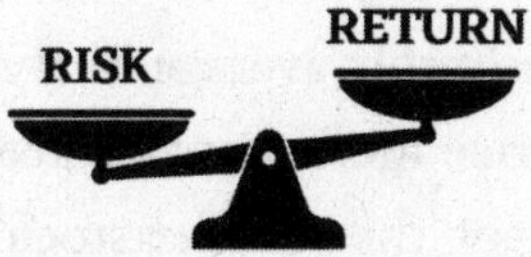

by rigorous academic research. For instance, David Blitz, Deputy Head of Quantitative Strategies at Robeco Asset Management in the Netherlands explained in a 2007 paper that equity investors overpay for risky stocks which are perceived to be similar to lottery tickets, with the aspiration to become rich,' Rohan elaborated.

'But these are overviews of technicalities. There are many caveats, conditions that need to be fulfilled for technical forecasts to become reality. Moreover, technical hypotheses are always contested. Therefore, rather than getting bogged down by the intricacies of mathematical models such as capital asset pricing model (of which beta is a component) and where they fail to deliver, let us just stick to the fundamental principle,' he suggested.

'The point, however, remains that you ought to be mindful of the time horizon while choosing your stock. A particular stock can very well be volatile in the short term, but the same stock over a longer term can turn out to be more stable (say 0.8 for monthly average over a four-year period). The price movement of 3M India, the Indian entity of the multinational conglomerate, perfectly exemplifies this point,' he continued.

'The short term picture (one year) appears to be very volatile. The price moving from Rs 21,111.25 on 6 January 2020 to Rs 21,100 on 1 January 2021, with a high of Rs 25,208.70 and a low of Rs 15,685.60. If you had bought the shares in January 2020, you would actually be on a lower level in January 2021. The picture, however, changes entirely when you look at a longer term (say five years). If you had bought the company's shares on 8 January 2016, you would have doubled your investment by January 2021. And, if you consider an even longer period, say January 2007, your investment would be 23 times bigger,' he pointed out.

'I see,' responded Vikram. He was listening intently, absorbing every word coming out of Rohan's mouth.

'For a contrasting picture, let us look at the Hindustan Construction Company, a company that has a long history in this country. Established in 1926 by the legendary Walchand Hirachand Doshi, who is credited for setting up India's first modern shipyard, first aircraft factory and first car factory, Hindustan Construction has come a long way. The company's revenue for 2019-20 was Rs 9,437.06 crore, compared to Rs 2,986.55 crore of 3M India,' Rohan said.

'However, the performance of the company's stock presents a very different picture. It went down marginally from Rs 10.10 on 6 January 2020 to Rs 9.10 on 1 January 2021 with a lot of volatility in between. Extending the time horizon to five or even fifteen years also does not change the picture substantially. For both periods, the performance of the stock is characterised by several cycles of sharp increases and declines. In fact, the stock price in January 2021 remains at a lower level than in January 2005. To be able to increase your investment in a stock like this, you would need to have exceptional abilities for predicting when it would reach the high point, in order to exit with profit,' he insisted.

Chapter 8

MIND THE DEBT

'Before you invest, be clear about a company's debt status,' Rohan warned. 'There are too many failure stories in the big league which have taken down many investors. Let us start with the story of Jet Airways,' he suggested.

As India's economy liberalised in the early 1990s, Jet Airways became a watch word for the success of a private enterprise. Starting operations in 1994, the airlines scaled new heights over the next two decades, expanding from domestic to international operations. The aviation sector in the county is one of the more difficult ones for the private sector, and competition for Jet toughened with the entry

of low cost carriers such as Indigo, GoAir and SpiceJet. To arrest its declining market share, Jet entered the low cost space by acquiring Air Sahara in 2007, rebranding it as JetLite. With its high quality service, increasing fleets and new routes, the story of Jet Airways continued to impress. At its peak, the company had 119 aircraft in its fleet and operated about 600 flights a day.

The growth story, however, got grounded by early 2019, when the company announced that it was indefinitely suspending all flights as it was running out of cash. Jet informed the stock exchanges that the company was unable to pay for fuel or other critical services to keep the operations going.

Reportedly, Jet Airways was incurring a daily loss of Rs 21 crore and its debt and dues amounted to Rs 15,000 crore. In February 2019, the company reported its fourth consecutive quarterly loss for the quarter ending December 2018. The company's market shares for domestic passengers dropped from 44 per cent in 2003-04 to 10 per cent in February 2019. Its share prices have fallen from Rs 1,100 (during its initial public offering) in February 2005 to Rs 24 in December 2019.

The crash defied logic. The company was one of the most respected private operators in India, and India's aviation sector had become one of the fastest growing in the world. How then could it fail? The long and short of the much discussed story is that the company could not manage its piling debts, a situation that was aggravated by operational losses. While the acquisition of Air Sahara curtailed its access to liquidity, Jet got a breather when Abu Dhabi's national carrier, Etihad Airways, bought a 24 per cent stake in 2013, allowing it to add new planes to its fleet to keep pace with growing demand. In mid-2018, Jet admitted that it had taken 300 mn US dollars in advance payments from lessors in the quarter ending June. By the end of November, the company had received default notices from the lessors. By the beginning of the next year, Jet defaulted on payments to a consortium of Indian banks, blaming a temporary cash flow mismatch. In the meantime, its efforts to raise more capital through mergers with other airlines and by selling more stake to Etihad failed to materialise. The company started grounding more and more planes and started defaulting on payments to employees.

Jet Airways founder and chairperson Naresh Goyal had to step down from the company's board in March 2019. And, after much uncertainty, the company's lenders approved a resolution plan submitted by a consortium comprising UK-based Kalrock Capital and UAE-based entrepreneur Murari Lal Jalan in October 2020 to revive the airline.

'Such a collapse is indeed shocking. I always liked their service,' confessed Vikram, becoming nostalgic about his pleasant experience on-board Jet Airways flights.

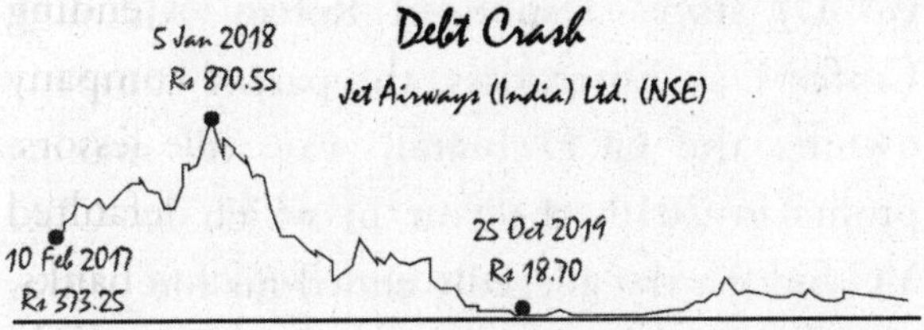

Source: Representative trend based on data sourced from Google Finance.

The story of Eveready, India's largest dry cell batteries manufacturers, is equally tragic. An increase in the company's valuation from Rs 210 crore in August 2013 to Rs 3,230 crore in January 2018 saw the number of pledged shares rise from 10.15 per cent to 88.51 percent. As markets came off and the company defaulted on its loan covenants, the lenders had no option but to sell pledged shares in the market. From the peak, the company has lost 87 per cent of its market value. But thankfully, the company is back on a growth path again.

'The most tragic outcome in this category

is perhaps that of Café Coffee Day,' argued Vikram. He sounded genuinely sad.

'True! Debt became one of the key reasons that brought an end to the Café Coffee Day (CCD) story,' responded Rohan. Although Coffee Day Enterprises, the parent company owning the CCD brand, was still making profits in 2019, the year in which its CEO VG Siddhartha allegedly ended his life, it was already in a debt trap. The company's leverage had sharply increased from Rs 3,688 crore in 2016 to Rs 6,547 in 2018, interest payments for which led to declining profitability. Over 70 per cent of the CEO's personal shares, who owned 32.75 per cent stake in the company were pledged or encumbered. The company had been raising capital from mutual funds by pledging more funds. It was in this situation that its talks for a sale to Blackstone of Tanglin Developments and a tie-up or sale to Coca Cola fell through.

'If I recall correctly, there are many more examples,' said Vikram. He tried to recollect the names. In the recent past, markets have seen firms such as the Reliance Group, Dewan Housing Finance Corporation Ltd (DHFL), and Infrastructure Leasing & Financial Services (ILFS) suffer similar fates. Their debts shot up to unmanageable levels, taking down the businesses. Selling controlling stake in Future Retail to Mukesh Ambani's RIL is seen as the biggest setback to Kishore Biyani, known to be one of India' best minds in the retail business. But how did he come to this point?

Future Group accrued a heavy debt over the years. As of September 30, 2019, debt at Future Group's listed entities rose to Rs 12,778 crore from Rs 10,951 crore as on March 31, 2019. The market buzz about his inability to service debt began in mid-February, sending group companies shares crashing, and triggering rating downgrades. Lenders sought more shares as collateral against loans to Biyani. The Coronavirus pandemic crippled the company's operations, and shutdowns of stores, and the subsequent cash crunch forced it to default on debts. Biyani became over ambitious in core retailing, and his focus on the neighbourhood format stores EasyDay, Nilgiris and Heritage backfired. He invested heavily on these ventures but they did not succeed. His excitement about the group's FMCG business, Future Consumer, proved particularly infectious. He dreamt of scaling up the Rs 2,000 crore business to Rs 20,000 crore by 2021. But the company faced losses, resulting in 11.24 per cent decline in its profit to Rs 619 crore in the first nine months of FY20. Future Retail defaulted on interest payments in July. Following suit, Future Consumer defaulted, followed by Future Enterprises' default on interest payment on non-convertible debentures. Biyani had no option but to sell his food and fashion retailing business, including Big Bazaar, fbb, Foodhall, Easyday, Nilgiris, Central and Brand Factory, besides the logistics and warehousing business, to Reliance Retail Ventures (RRVL).

Biyani's struggle with debt has a long history. In FY12, he was in an identical Rs 12,000 crore debt soup, which forced him to sell his most valuable asset, Pantaloons Retail, to the Aditya Birla group for Rs 1,600 crore.

That journey, too, hit a roadblock in March, when shares of Future Group companies lost significant value, leading to ratings downgrade of the promoter holding company and invocation of pledged shares by lenders. He also sold Future Capital to Warburg Pincus for Rs 4,250 crore.

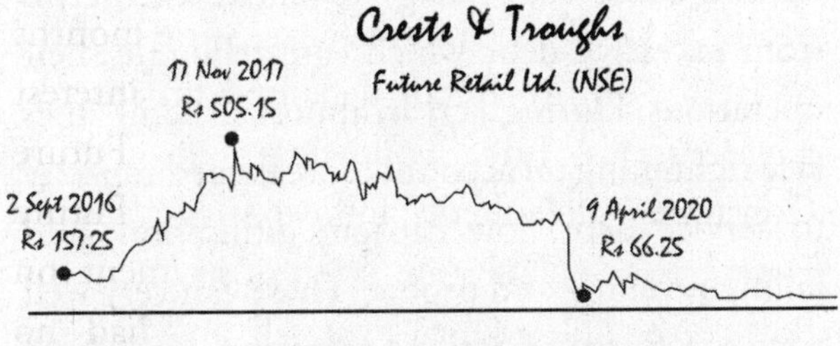

Source: Representative trend based on data sourced from Google Finance.

'I remember that during the pandemic, the GVK Group, too, had to sell its stake in the Mumbai International Airport to Adani. Wockhardt has sold part of its domestic branded formulations division to Dr Reddy's Laboratories Ltd, and GMR Infrastructure divested its entire stake in Kakinada SEZ to Aurobindo Realty and Infrastructure,' Vikram said, adding to the already long list. Other prominent companies that have faced the heat of the debt burden include Essar Steel, Bhushan Steel, Bhushan Power and Steel, Jaypee Infratech, Jaiprakash Associates, Lanco Infratech, Amtek Auto, Videocon Industries, and Binani Cement.

On the other side, many companies take it up as a conscious strategy to shield themselves from excessive debt which can debilitate their operations. During a crisis, almost all companies face tightening on account of weakened capacity to service debt, low capacity utilisation, and falling revenues and profits. These can very well trigger a flurry of actions ranging from sale of assets/stakes, shutting down stressed businesses, frenetic fund raising, and sharp, almost brutal, reduction in costs. This has particularly hurt firms with high debt and low interest coverage ratio (ICR), which measures how many times a company's earnings can cover current interest payments. Those with low ICR include giants such as Anil Agarwal's Vedanta Ltd, Gautam Adani's Adani Power and Sunil Mittal's Bharti Airtel. Many of them can tide over the crisis

> The **INTEREST COVERAGE RATIO** is a debt and profitability ratio used to determine how easily a company can pay interest on its outstanding debt.
>
> Source: Investopedia

with support from other group companies and assets. L&T, for example, plans to reduce its Rs 1.24 lakh crore debt by Rs 30,000 crore by March 2021 by selling L&T Infrastructure Development Projects and Nabha Power and transferring its Hyderabad Metro stake to an investment trust. However, further worsening of the economic environment could spell trouble for the giants, too.

Consider the case of Tata Motors. The company's ICR turned negative in March 2020. In a post Covid review in June, Moody's downgraded its debt by a few notches. The automotive division is saddled with Rs 67,800 crore debt. Its net debt to equity ratio rose from 0.84 in June 2019 to 1.44 in June 2020. Although Tata Group Chairman

N Chandrasekaran has targeted making the company net debt free in three years, credit rating agencies are sceptical.

'It is needless to emphasise that higher debt can add an element of volatility to earnings due to additional interest expense. It can also increase a company's vulnerability to business downturns. As economists will tell you, not all debt is bad. In fact, borrowings are critical to the expansion of businesses. Moreover, cost of debt (which is the interest cost) is considered to be lower than the cost of equity (which includes the return to shareholders). Thus, taking recourse to debt can reduce the average cost of capital. It is therefore important to distinguish between useful debt—borrowings that can fuel growth, and bad debt—when

> *The **COST OF DEBT** is the effective interest rate that a company pays on its debts, such as bonds and loans. It can refer to the before-tax cost of debt or the after-tax cost of debt.*
>
> *Source: Investopedia*

> *The **COST OF EQUITY** is the return that a company requires to decide if an investment meets capital return requirements.*
>
> *Source: Investopedia*

a company borrows more to keep existing businesses alive and service existing debts. Tata Motors is the perfect case of a company whose stress was already high but got aggravated due to demand collapse post Covid.

'At this point, I'd like to ask you about a technical term because I see it being widely used by investment advisors. Moreover, since we are discussing debt, it is important to have clarity on it. How should an individual investor deal with the debt-equity ratio?' Vikram asked Rohan.

'Debt-equity ratio (D/E ratio) is the metric used to measure the extent of the debt of companies so that they can be compared on a uniform scale. In simple terms, it tells you how much debt or liability a company has for every rupee of funds owned by shareholders.

$$\textbf{DEBT-EQUITY RATIO (D/E RATIO)} = \frac{\textbf{TOTAL LIABILITIES}}{\textbf{SHAREHOLDER EQUITY}}$$

D/E ratio also tells you whether shareholder equity can cover outstanding debts in the situation of a business downturn,' he explained.

'There is no ideal figure for this ratio, but it should neither be too high nor too low. If the ratio is too high, it shows that a company may be in financial distress and unable to pay its debtors. On the other hand, if it is too low, that implies that a company is over dependent on equity to finance its business, making it costly and inefficient,' he further noted.

Moreover, the ratio varies widely across industry sectors. Some researchers are of the opinion that technology-based businesses usually have a ratio of two or below, large manufacturing and stable publicly traded companies have ratios between two and five, whereas financial businesses can see it go up to ten or even twenty. Data from the Organisation for Economic Co-operation and Development (OECD) countries shows that these figures can vary significantly across geographies too.

One estimate from India that studied 132 companies distributed across twenty different industries in 2016 found that the D/E ratio of these companies was in the range of 0.0046 to 8.2379. The software industry had the lowest ratio, and the banking sector, the highest. Contrary to the common perception that large cap companies have higher D/E ratio (due to their established business and familiarity with lenders), the study found that the average ratio of small cap companies was more than large and mid-cap companies. These findings should alert retail investors to be mindful about possible higher risks in small cap companies.

'What about the interest coverage ratio?' asked Vikram.

'The interest coverage ratio shows a company's earnings before taxes as a proportion of its interest payments. A ratio of two, for instance, indicates that a company generates Rs 2 for every rupee in interest expense. Naturally, a lower ratio will tell you that a company might be in trouble,' Rohan replied.

'Yet, despite the apparent benefits of debt, there is no denying that it increases the risk. During a high growth period, debt can help increase shareholder returns, but the story changes when the going gets tough. In a tough economic situation, where liquidity becomes a pain point, it is almost certain that companies which are already highly leveraged will be the first ones to feel the heat. In India, the two periods of 2003-2007 which saw a high phase of economic growth, and the low growth phase of the post global financial crisis are clear examples of this difference. Therefore, it is a better option for investors to put their money in companies with strong balance sheets, with negligible, if not zero debt. Besides, the phenomenon of debt reflects a negative social ethos which ultimately reflects on the image of leveraged companies. The returns, as a consequence, tend to be lower than debt-free companies,' he noted.

'Can we be sure that all will be well with a zero debt company?' queried Vikram. He wanted to be clear.

'Let me reemphasize that I am proposing the zero debt status of a company only as one of many filters. Being zero debt does not guarantee superb performance or returns. A recent study, for example, analysed the performance of zero debt companies in 2019 and noticed that the record is mixed. The study had considered only those stocks that have market capitalisation greater than Rs 500 crore, of which there are close to 160 zero debt stocks across various sectors listed on bourses. Out of these 160 stocks, it found that 71 zero debt stocks had yielded positive returns in 2019. The average return for all the zero debt stocks was approximately three per cent. However, the zero debt companies from sectors such as finance, capital goods, healthcare, consumer durables and insurance sector were found to have performed comparatively better,' Rohan elaborated.

'It does seem to be a wonderful strategy to invest in zero debt companies but it is not logical to simply include the zero debt companies in the portfolio just because they are zero debt companies. Debt actually is a lower cost source of funds for any company. What investors are looking for is optimal growth. In a strong economic growth outlook and a lower interest rate regime, a company can actually use leverage to add capacity and grow optimally. In spite of a strong vision of the growth, if the company adopts a low leverage option, there are chances that it may lose market share to its competitor. A proactive strategy may be required in a growing economy to tap growth optimally. Optimal leverage in such conditions helps tap growth opportunities, and zero debt companies may underperform in such a market environment,' he remarked.

'Moreover, zero debt companies may lose out on the tax shield. Another well documented disadvantage of being a zero debt company is management discipline. It is observed that leveraged companies are likely to be more disciplined in their expenditure, when compared to those companies that enjoy higher cash flows and higher income. Complacency can kick in for zero debt companies when compared to a leveraged company, which may lead to unwarranted expenses and inefficiencies. Therefore, even after selecting zero debt companies, you will have to make sure that they pass through the other filters,' he stressed.

'The biggest positive of having a zero debt stock in the portfolio is that these stocks have little exposure to interest rate risks, and they are insulated from any rise in borrowing cost. Also, the low interest outgo for zero debt companies allows the company to retain more cash. The excess cash can be strategically used for tapping growth prospects or for distributing dividends. It is quite possible that zero debt companies enjoy a scarcity premium over their leveraged peers. It is possible to see several multinational companies (MNC) feature in the list of zero debt companies. In the current environment, with no meaningful cut in interest rates expected for a few quarters, and given a low growth environment, companies with low debt or companies that are debt free should be preferred for investments. While investors can and should consider the quality of debt free companies to be included in the portfolio, there is no guarantee that a company will outperform simply because it is debt free. Just because a debt free company has better chances of survival in the downturn, that does not mean that it will outperform when the market condition reverses. Investors should consider all other parameters such as consistent growth in profits and sales over the past few years before making any investment decisions. Preference can be given to those debt free stocks that operate in a growing industry. For example, if the outlook for the capital goods sector is positive, identifying the debt free companies in the capital goods sector can be profitable. Debt free companies do have an advantage but only a limited one,' he insisted.

'Let me come to the question that I cannot stop myself from asking,' confessed Vikram. He looked impatient. 'Does increased debt really have an effect on a company's stock performance?' he asked.

'A 2009 paper by scholars from Philadelphia's Drexel University and Singapore Management University, who studied the performance of US stocks between 1975 and 2002 in relation with their leverage ratio showed that it does,' Rohan informed Vikram. 'The study showed that a change in a firm's leverage ratio has a significantly negative impact on its stock prices. In addition, firms that increase their leverage ratio tend to have lower investments in future,' he clarified.

'In India, companies with lower levels of debt have usually outperformed those with higher debt. Companies like Infosys, TCS, Bosch, Siemens, 3M, HDFC Life, Honeywell Automation and Oracle, which have virtually no debt or extremely low D/E ratio, have done very well in the stock markets. The trend also shows that stocks in sectors such as steel, infrastructure and real estate began performing better after companies cut down their debt,' Rohan illustrated.

'Yet another study looked at all the companies listed on the Sensex BSE 500 and picked those that have been decreasing levels of total debt on the books continuously since 2016. Most companies that fit the bill showed an increasing trend in profit levels over the years. Despite the slowdown, companies such as Relaxo Footwear, IPCA Laboratories and Vaibhav Global gave stock returns in excess of 50 percent,' he went on before asking,

'This session should have completed your information gathering on all the filters?' He smiled, although he was visibly exhausted, having talked for hours.

'I'm almost done,' replied Vikram. He was a bit hesitant to press further, but it was important to get the final filter clarified. 'It will be very useful if you could share why you put entire industry sectors out of your investment purview. What makes them the untouchables?' Vikram asked.

Chapter 9

THE AVOIDABLES

'There are certain types of stocks that I always avoid,' admitted Rohan. Perhaps, he, too, wanted to be done with explaining the filter framework. 'I can broadly put them into two groups, not that these companies are bad or that they always underperform. However, they can seriously dent your path to wealth creation in a steady manner for the sectors to which they belong,' he added.

'The first component of this "avoidable" category is commodity stocks,' he announced.

'Commodities are known to be risky investment propositions. This is because the market movement is determined by demand and supply, which are, in turn, influenced by uncertainties. These are difficult, if not impossible to predict, such as unusual weather patterns, epidemics, and disasters, both natural and man-made; fluctuating production levels (of which oil is a particularly hazardous one), and government policies. Traders involved in commodity trading are aware of their probability of incurring either massive losses or huge profits. The huge gains that result from trading commodities can come paired with the adverse risk of losing out on all of the money,' Rohan observed.

'Moreover, due to a greater risk of rallies and crashes, the commodities market is a lot more susceptible to speculations in comparison to the stock market. Hence, an investor must be ready to incur potential losses in the case of any adversities. As you can well imagine, this is something that individual investors should scrupulously avoid,' he cautioned.

'What about the other category that you have included? The stocks of those companies that produce goods which are considered social evils?' asked Vikram.

'Yes, particularly alcoholic drinks and tobacco,' Rohan insisted. 'Don't get me wrong. These are not my value judgements, but those that come from society in general and from the government, in particular,' he added.

'Even a college kid knows that governments—both Central and the states—actively discourage the consumption of these products. A global war is waging against the tobacco industry. Now, an Australian not for profit, Tobacco Free Portfolios (TFP), is trying to hit where it hurts the most: Cut off finance to tobacco companies. Since August 2018,

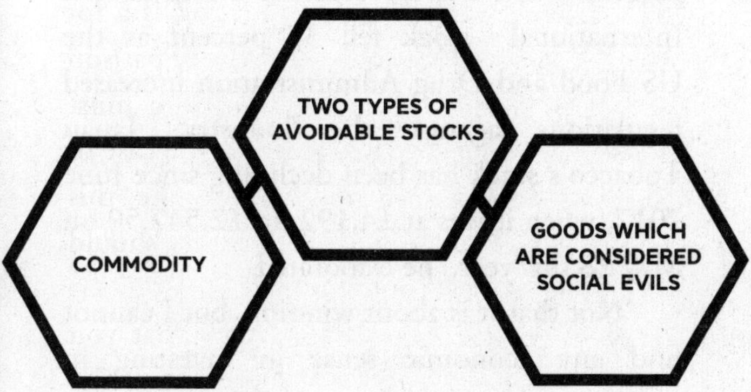

TFP has convinced over 100 banking, financial service and insurance [BFSI] companies to sign a pledge to review their position on investing in tobacco manufacturers. The 109 signatories of the Tobacco-Free Finance Pledge represent over $9.5 trillion worth of assets under management (AUM), corporate loan book, and insurance premiums actively under review. BNP Paribas Asset Management's AUM worth €200 billion is tobacco-free. A founding signatory of the pledge, the company's position extends to all group entities, including subsidiaries, affiliates, and joint ventures. According to Bloomberg news, British American Tobacco had its worst year in 2018, with its stock falling 50 percent, while Marlboro maker Philip Morris International's stock fell 37 percent as the US Food and Drug Administration increased regulations against the industry. Japan Tobacco's stock has been declining since June 2017, when it was at £4,192, to £2,547.50 on May 28 this year,' he elaborated.

'Not that it is about winning, but I cannot find any economic sense in investing in products that are constantly being penalised, and whose growth prospects are doomed,' expressed Rohan. 'Remember that the global anti-tobacco campaign is unhappy not because the tobacco industry is growing, but because the number of consumers is not reducing fast enough,' he stated.

'India may have one of the largest markets for these products, but that's purely because of its population size and traditional habits. Make no mistake. The consumer base of tobacco is declining. And, the government's attitude towards alcohol is so frivolous that you never know where and when it is going to be banned,' announced Rohan, and then, he stopped talking. He was completely exhausted.

Chapter 10

LOOKOUT FOR THE NEW AGE COMPANIES

Vikram had a sneaking feeling that the chef's secret had left out one crucial element of modern economy—the new age technology-driven companies, mostly start-ups, that were going to soon get listed. The most important among these are companies that have been named asset light companies. How does one evaluate them?

He sat down again at his work station at home in the still of the night. This question had been bothering him for some time, and he hadn't yet discussed it with anyone. Vikram decided to look for the answers himself.

A couple of hours into his research, he realised that this topic was more complicated that he had presumed. It was going to take him days to get a comprehensive picture.

After seven consecutive nights of research, Vikram felt that he had been able to touch upon the essentials of this category. At the end of it, he put together his findings and views in the form of a note, and started reading it from the beginning.

That technology is changing the world, is cliché. Technology has been changing lives since the dawn of human civilisation, but new technologies such as the internet and artificial intelligence have accelerated the pace of change in a manner that was probably unforeseeable even in the last century. It has opened up new avenues for all components of our society. From smart manufacturing, logistics, smart cities, smart homes, medical care and consumer services to education, there is barely any aspect of our lives that is not being transformed rapidly by the application of new technologies.

Among the many things that technology

has done and continues to do, probably the most important is disrupting the old ways of doing business. Of course, the twentieth century saw the technological revolution ushered in by IBM, Microsoft, Apple and similar companies, but their innovations were focussed on new products and processes. It was only in the last decade of the past century that a company was incorporated, which started reshaping the business landscape. Tomes have been written about how Amazon has changed the way we shop, and given new weight to the word 'e-commerce'. Remarkably, it wasn't the first one in the field to dominate the space. However, its relentless innovation and expansion of the scale of business has dwarfed what happened before it arrived. By one estimate, Amazon IPO shares in 1997 worth a hundred US dollars would be valued at 120,000 dollars today.

Jeff Bezos, the founder of Amazon, found his opportunity in the internet. 'I came across this startling statistic that web usage was growing at 2300% a year. So, I decided I would try and find a business plan that made sense in the context of that growth, and I picked books as the first best product to sell online,' Bezos had told the American public broadcaster and television program distributor Public Broadcasting Service (PBS).

Another company that made its presence felt with a somewhat similar model was eBay. Founded in 1995, a year after Amazon, and initially named AuctionWeb (the name was changed in 1997), eBay used the auction style for consumer to consumer sales.

The story can be found to be reflected in Japan, too. In 2018, Tokyo-based Mercari, a Japanese e-commerce company, founded in February 2013, and currently operating in Japan and the United States, pulled in 324 million dollars in sales, taking a 10 per cent cut of every transaction. Founder Shintaro Yamada's 32 per cent stake in the firm climbed up to 1.3 billion dollars. The company's stock has zigzagged upward since its June 2018 IPO. "Our mission: To create new value" Yamada told Forbes Japan in November. "We've had a pretty good response" ever since Mercari was founded in 2013. Yamada's boldest move was probably to take on eBay directly. Within 14 months of starting Mercari in Japan, he launched in America, a market that represents only 6 per cent of its business. Yamada expressed indifference as to whether the gambit will pay off.

Apart from every other innovation used to evolve their businesses, what these companies have pioneered is the model that has come to be known as asset light business. Although Amazon has its own warehouses where products are stored and shipped, the company never owned shops the way we know traditional retail. Moreover, by 2017, items sold by third party sellers accounted for more than Amazon's direct sales.

This basically means that Amazon is now trading more goods that it sells. eBay, on the other hand, only provides the platform for transactions. It was only in 2019 that the company started rolling out its plan for providing warehousing and shipping services to facilitate faster shipping for eBay sellers.

The trend of companies being asset light has only grown stronger in the past few years. An increasing number of companies is taking its services to customers without owning physical assets, thus significantly reducing traditional business risks and improving profitability. As one article in the Harvard Business Review of claimed in September 2016, "Investors today prefer companies with fewer physical assets".

Barry Libert and Megan Beck, a board member and chief products and insights officer at OpenMatters, a machine learning company, along with Yoram (Jerry) Wind, a professor of marketing at the University of Pennsylvania's Wharton School argued that the industrial age model of equating more physical assets (raw materials, properties, plants, and equipment) with greater value had undergone a transition in the digital age where "the physical assets that the big industrial companies have acquired are becoming more and more burdensome". In a fast changing operating environment, the challenges of owning and maintaining and upgrading inventory and equipment, and acquiring land "are preventing companies from adapting, and weighing them down".

In order to find out whether asset light companies perform better than traditional industrial companies, the authors analysed the 1,500 companies listed on the S&P1500 index, which is a mix of small, medium, and large-cap stocks in the US, categorised into industry sectors. They used two parameters to determine the relationship: (a) each industry's average Net PP&E (property, plant, and equipment) as a percentage of total assets, and (b) each industry's average revenue multiple, measuring how highly companies are valued in relation to their revenue.

The conclusion of the study is fascinating: the industries with the lowest percentage of physical assets were those with the highest revenue multiples.

Industries such as utilities, energy, transportation, and retail, for which PP&E account for more than 30 per cent of total assets, were found to have multiple below two.

DID YOU KNOW?

PP&E stands for Property, Plant, and Equipment

Average PP&E accounted for less than 20 per cent for another group of service provider industries, such as consumer goods, health services, electronic technology and distribution services. Although these industries have low PP&E per cent share, they are still restricted by their use of assets which are "non-scalable," such as human resources. As a result, despite being comparatively asset light, their multiples, too, remained below two.

It was the third category, which was found to have both low PP&E per cent share and multiples above two. This category included industries such as technology services and health technology, which the authors claimed to have "highly scalable, and highly desirable, intangible assets". They also found the financial services industry to display similar characteristics, but noted that their high multiple levels found in this exercise was chiefly due to the inclusion of real estate investment trusts (REITs), which pay out high dividends to investors.

Similar results were found by the consulting firm Boston Consulting Group (BCG) in 2014, when it analysed the financial results of 2,687 of the largest companies across 24 industry sectors. Industries that have lower levels of assets generate a better return on the assets they hold, the analysis concluded.

According to the BCG analysis, the ratio of market value of equity to operating assets is better for asset light companies than for their peers in almost every sector. Profits of higher asset-owning companies are also more volatile as their net income depends on the ability to recover the high fixed cost for assets. Asset light companies' profits, in contrast, are less volatile as their costs are more flexible, relative to their revenues. Companies with lower levels of asset ownership also respond faster to changing demands, technology advancements, new market opportunities, and supply chain disruptions. Asset light models can help companies achieve scale without having to invest capital.

For instance, the production of semiconductors typically requires multibillion dollar capital investments, which very few companies have the scale to justify. Intel owns its own fabrication plants, but Apple takes the asset light route, buying many of its chips from Taiwan Semiconductor Manufacturing Company, as do many smaller companies that aim to minimize the amount of capital tied up in fixed assets. Utilisation of fixed assets being critical for revenue generation, some companies also share them. For instance, Cathay Pacific and DHL share aircraft to provide combined passenger and cargo flights. Yet another way to remain asset light is through licensing, whereby a company licenses the use of its product to a partner, sometimes in another industry. Armani Hotels & Resorts, for example, licensed its brand to Dubai-based Emaar Properties in 2004 as a way to participate in the luxury hotel market without actually buying properties.

In today's business environment, it is not just scalability, but the speed of scaling up that is crucial in deciding a company's fate in the market. It is, therefore, important to be nimble and on your feet, so that you can either lead the change in a dynamic market environment or be able to respond to it quickly. This can only be possible if you leverage technology effectively. Technology makes you less reliant on people, and offers quick and accurate insights into

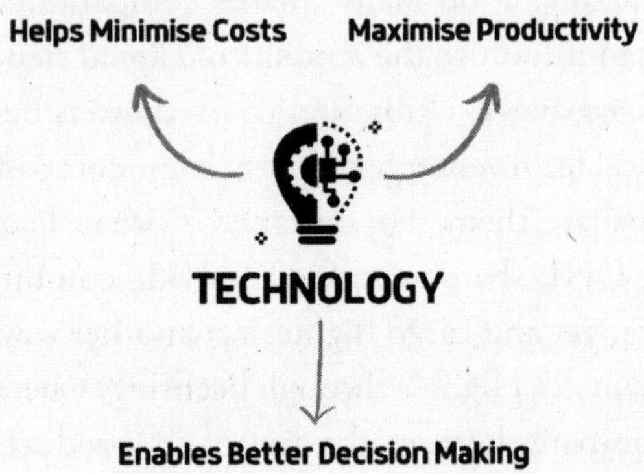

different aspects of the business. It, therefore, helps minimise costs and maximise productivity, and enables better decision making.

The world of e-commerce has expanded phenomenally in recent times and is slated for faster growth in the years to come. By one estimate, e-retail sales worldwide in 2017 amounted to 2.3 trillion US dollars, which is projected to grow to 4.88 trillion dollars in 2021. The growth potential of this segment is clear from the fact that the top ten global e-commerce retailers (Amazon.com, JD.com, Suning Commerce Group, Apple, Walmart, Dell Technologies, Vipshop Holdings, Otto Group, Gome Electrical Appliances and Macy's) account for only 15 per cent of all global ecommerce. More importantly, e-retail sales that accounted for 14.1 per cent of all retail sales worldwide in 2019 is expected to reach 22 per cent in 2023. This phenomenon is possible due to the central role of technology.

It is no wonder, therefore, that technology companies are at the forefront of the line of giant asset light companies. Seven out of the world's ten largest companies by market capitalisation are technology companies, which include Microsoft, Apple, Amazon, Alphabet and Facebook. The other remarkable fact is that except Microsoft and Apple, these companies are not more than twenty-five years old.

One of the most prominent examples of how a company leveraged technology to transform its existing business is that of Netflix. Started in 1997 as a DVD sales and rental business in 1997, the company's innovative mail order service virtually ended the bricks and mortar rental shop model of businesses like Blockbuster, which filed for bankruptcy protection in 2010. Netflix expanded to streaming media, a decade after it started business. By July 2020, it had become the largest entertainment/media company by market capitalisation, displacing competitors like Walt Disney, AT&T and Comcast. In the recent years, a number of players have flocked to the asset light and technology driven growth market of streaming over-the-top platforms such as Amazon Prime Video, HBO Max,

NBCUniversal's Peacock, Discovery+, Apple TV+, Walt Disney's (DIS) Disney+, and Hulu. In India, the new entrants include ZEE5, SonyLiv, Voot, AltBalaji, among others.

There is another story of the prevalence of new age technology and asset light models over the traditional asset heavy ones in the bankruptcy of Hertz, one of America's largest car rental companies, in May 2020. The company had a debt burden of about 19 billion dollars. And, its nearly 700,000 vehicles (cars that it had bought and leased from carmakers) largely idled because of the situation created by the coronavirus pandemic. The market for the used cars that Hertz sold after retiring them from its fleet, declined steeply. The pandemic might have been responsible for bringing the curtain down on this tale, but experts point out that the rot had set in much earlier. *Forbes* attributed the failure of the company to its inertia and inability to recognise the fast changing trends and a refusal to adapt its business models accordingly. Hertz was not the only one to be hurt. Advantage Rent A

Car, another car rental company, also went bankrupt in May. Avis, another big player in the US car rental market, rebounded from the slowdown by cutting down its fleet by a fourth; through cost savings, job cuts and by raising 500 mn dollars from debt investors at a high interest rate. Across the Atlantic, Paris based Europcar faced a similar fate.

When traditional car rental companies were struggling to keep their head above the water, the footprints of their new age competitors, in contrast, were steadily increasing across the world. As the automobile industry went into a prolonged slump in 2019, India's Finance Minister Nirmala Sitharaman cited the preference of millennials for taxi aggregators like Ola and Uber instead of committing for monthly instalments to own a car as a key reason. Whether her explanation was correct or not is not relevant to our discussion. What is undeniable is the great extent to which urban India has come to depend on services provided by Ola and Uber.

Founded in 2009, Uber uses its technology

platform to simply connect passengers with taxis. It doesn't own the cars, nor are the drivers its employees. By the time it went public in May 2019, it was valued at a staggering 82.4 bn dollars. Only Alibaba, the Chinese e-commerce company, which went public in 2014 at 168 bn dollars, and Facebook, which was at 104 bn dollars when it went public in 2012, had seen anything bigger than this. In 2019, the company was present in over ten thousand cities in 69 countries, with 111 mn customers, who used its services at least once a month, amounting to 7 bn trips. A couple of months before Uber's IPO, another app-based ridesharing Lyft had gone public with a valuation of 24.3 billion dollars. In November 2020, Uber commanded a market share of 70 percent and Lyft 30 percent in the US.

Uber started its India operations from Bangalore in August 2013 and had expanded to more than sixty cities by early 2020. India, however, has had its own versions of ridesharing companies, the earliest of which is Meru Cabs, set up in 2006. Although Meru started off by owning all the cars in its fleets, it started moving towards being asset light by adding cars owned by drivers to its fleet. By 2014, half its cars were owned by drivers. To synergise its operations, Meru has gone on to tie up with companies like e-retailer Flipkart and travel company MakeMyTrip for grocery deliveries and dedicated airport services. Meru still remains an unlisted company, but its long term potential is underscored by the acquisition of 55 per cent of its shares by Mahindra & Mahindra in 2019 at an investment of Rs 103 cr (approximately 14 mn dollars).

Sharp growth has also been registered by Ola Cabs, an app-based cab aggregator company that started its operations only ten years ago in 2010 and was valued reportedly at 6.2 bn in 2019. Starting out from Mumbai, the company now operates in over 150 cities across India, UK, Australia and New Zealand, serving more than 150 mn users, and completing over a billion rides annually. The Indian companies have not escaped the squeeze on the ride-hailing segment by the travel bans due to the corona virus pandemic, but the growth potential of a large, untapped market, and the adaptability of the asset light companies are keeping the optimistic outlook alive. Although the market size is estimated to have dropped nearly by half in 2020 to 19.7 bn dollars from the previous year, analysts project that it is not only going to rebound soon, but that it is expected to increase to 55.4 bn dollars by 2025, with 25 mn new users added.

Similar shifts are taking place in other sectors, as well. In the hospitality segment, Airbnb revolutionised the travel and tourism stay business. Hotels were no more the only option. Airbnb's online platform directly connected travellers to people who wanted to rent out their properties. The company didn't have to own any property. Founded in 2008, Airbnb went public in December 2020 with a valuation of 100 bn dollars. To put things in perspective, that is twice the value of Marriott, the largest hotel chain in the world. Marriott has been in business since 1927.

Starting its operations in 2016, Airbnb

quickly expanded to 54,000 listings on its platform in India across more than 100 cities. It is so bullish on its future prospects in the Indian market that it expects India to become one of its top three markets in the long run.

In India, something similar has been done by Oyo Hotels and Homes. Founded in 2013, Oyo started as a hotel aggregator, which leased some rooms and sold them under its brand name. Later, it transitioned to a franchise model, where it partnered with hotels and vacation homes, selling their rooms which are standardised to its hospitality services guidelines to customers at competitive prices. In a short span of seven years, Oyo expanded its operations to over 800 cities in 80 countries with more than a million rooms in 43,000 hotels. The number of vacation homes for travellers with which the company tied up increased to over 130,000 homes around the world. By mid-2019, the company claimed that it had climbed to the position of the world's third largest hotel chain.

All these are impressive growth stories that

reflect the overall growth story of asset light companies, particularly those which are built on digital platforms. Typically, these companies bring together two or more market actors and grow through network effects. When a study by MIT Sloan analysed a 2017 list of more than 200 start-ups with valuations of 1 bn dollars billion or more, the researchers found that 60-70 per cent of them were platform businesses. This, according to researchers, demonstrates the popularity of such businesses among entrepreneurs and private investors.

However, everything about this picture is not as rosy as it appears. Despite having a number of inherent advantages, these companies still have to negotiate fundamental business challenges to prove their long term viability. They have to prove that they are not only economically superior, but that they are also politically and socially viable. They have to manoeuvre deftly between government regulations, workers' issues and their social image. It is fair to point out that most of the companies discussed here have faced strong challenges on these counts.

But from the business point of view, what is most challenging for these businesses is to achieve profitability and grow it. The big question that an investor faces, is whether to invest in these companies, although they have scaled up their businesses at an unprecedented pace. Companies like Uber, Lyft, Spotify, Slack and AirBnB are all running in losses. In India, however, Uber has been making profits. Oyo's internal projections reportedly show that it is unlikely to make profits in India and China until 2022.

Let us try to understand the phenomenon in a little more detail with the example of Uber. Many experts and analysts have strongly discouraged investing in the company. For instance, writing in Forbes, Stephen McBride, the editor of the RiskHedge Report opined that Uber is trapped in a money-losing spiral that it cannot escape. Gad Allon, Wharton professor of operations, information and decisions, and director of the Jerome Fisher Program in Management and Technology, on the other hand, wasn't too worried about the losses. He argued that many tech giants like Facebook, too, didn't do well in the initial phase, and that they started performing well much later. Indeed, Facebook turned profitable five years after being founded, Amazon after nearly a decade, and Twitter after twelve years. His concern is that subsidising drivers and passengers has been a key strategy of Uber's growth. He wonders whether the company will be able to overcome that trajectory to achieve profitability. Uber has made no secret that with its operational expenses set to increase significantly, it does not foresee profitability in the near future.

David Erickson, Wharton lecturer and former co-head of global equity capital markets at Barclays, has a different take. He bets on the future of Uber, which he calls a transformative technology company, because he believes that Uber will innovate and focus more on synergistic activities. In fact, the company already offers meal delivery, freight, electric bikes and scooters, self-driving vehicles and urban aviation. According to Erickson, the network effect created by the loss-making, hail-riding operations will be replaced by other elements that will ride on its strong platform to transform into quite a different company than what it is now. To categorise Uber just as a ridesharing platform is to undervalue the company "which has the DNA to become a game changing consumer distribution ecosystem". Such transformations have been the characteristic features of most tech giants such as Google, Amazon and Facebook, which have diversified over time, and look very different from the time they started out.

Optimism notwithstanding, there are some real challenges faced by the technology platform-based companies that should be kept in mind before including them in your portfolio. In their article in the Harvard Business Review in May 2019, professors David B Yoffie from the Harvard Business School, Annabelle Gawer from the University of Surrey and Michael A Cusumano from MIT Sloan, presented some striking findings to explain both the upside and the downside of these kind of firms.

Yoffie, Gawer and Cusumano identified 43 publicly-listed platform companies in the Forbes Global 2000 data for twenty years. They found that these companies generated the same level of annual revenues as their non-platform counterparts, but used half the number of employees. They had twice the operating profits and much higher market values and growth rates. The darker side of the picture was that they also found 209 American platform-based companies that had competed with the 43 companies, but failed. In other words, the number of failures was nearly five times the number of success stories. According to the authors, the failure stemmed from factors such as mispricing, failure to develop trust with users and partners, prematurely dismissing the competition, and entering the market too late.

In the meantime, technology start-ups are proliferating in India at an astonishing rate and are successful in raising funds in high volumes. These start-ups in India raised 14.5 billion dollars in 2019, up from 550 million dollars in 2010, a straight 25 times increase in a decade. The only time they raised more money was in 2017 when the figure was about 15 billion dollars. Nearly 1,900 start-ups were founded during the year, and close to 900 of them were funded. Two deals raised a billion dollars or more each. Hotel booking provider Oyo Rooms raised 1.5 billion dollars, while mobile wallet and financial services provider Paytm raised 1 billion dollars.

Udaan, a B2B online commerce platform provider, raised 585 million dollars while Delhivery, a logistics provider for e-commerce businesses, raised 413 million dollars. Among the investors, the top five most active venture capital firms were Sequoia Capital, Accel, Tiger Global Management, Blume Ventures and Chiratae Ventures. The most active private equity firms were Steadview Capital, General Atlantic, FMO, Sabre Partners India and CDC Group. "The range of companies and sectors that are active today has broadened and deepened," according to Dev Khare, a partner at Lightspeed Venture Partners. The ecosystem, too, has grown.

But are they able to step into the profit zone?

The wholesale and marketplace entities at Amazon India cumulatively posted losses of about Rs 5,800 crore in FY19, while at Walmart-owned Flipkart, losses at the corresponding units stood at about Rs 5,460 crore. Both companies have seen their revenue surge, but growth seems to have come at a cost. Amazon launched in India six years ago while Flipkart has been in the fray for about 12 years. This is reminiscent of the early days of Amazon in the US, where it began as an online bookstore in 1994.

Amazon posted its first profit of about 5 million dollars in the fourth quarter of 2001, after being in the business for about seven years. By that yardstick, Amazon in India is inching close to that timeline but Flipkart is well past that. For both Flipkart and Amazon, churning profits seems like a distant dream, at least in the near future, according to market analysts.

In the early days of e-commerce in India,

Amazon and Flipkart, along with the likes of Snapdeal, Paytm Mall and ShopClues, tried attracting consumers with offers and discounts. This was done with the intent to get shoppers into the habit of buying online. The online retailers have followed the model of discount-driven approach to gain market share. At the same time, they continued to invest in strengthening their logistics and supply chain networks. That explains their need for raising fresh investments to meet the huge upfront expenses, to a great extent. Besides, mobile phones continue to remain the largest category for ecommerce companies.

However, it is a low margin business, and doesn't add significantly to the bottom line. The companies also need to make significant investments to expand the market. The low penetration of online retail in India means total customers haven't yet reached a big number for a market like India. Once this changes to a scenario where more buyers flock in to shop online and spend more, these companies will start making profits. That might take a few more years but the trend is clear.

In the final analysis, I reiterate that asset light businesses, especially the platform-based ones hold out great hope, but by no means, guarantee success. Therefore, when India's top internet firms go for their IPO in the near future, you will need to pause and think before jumping onto the bandwagon. The companies that are expected to go public in the next two to three years include Flipkart, Paytm, Byju's, PhonePe, Zomato, Policybazar, Delhivery, BigBasket, OYO, and Ola. Before investing in them, you must judge whether they pass the cautionary principles discussed in this chapter as well as the filter framework that this book presents.

Did you ever pay attention to these cautionary principles before?

Chapter 11

STAY TUNED TO THE SIGNALS OF CHANGE

"An investment in knowledge pays the best interest" Benjamin Franklin is supposed to have said three hundred years ago. His sage advice holds true even today. I would, however, add that for wise investments, keep your antennae fine-tuned and alert. Observe, absorb and process information to make the best decisions on where to invest.

Making predictions is tough. But think of the venture capital and private equity firms. The key element of their operations is to spot a pattern before it becomes a trend, and then to pick probable winners. One can argue that they enjoy the cushion for trial and error due to the huge amount of funds at their disposal and the wide variety of firms they invest in. That makes it possible to hedge a lot of their investments. A retail investor does not enjoy that luxury. That is precisely my argument. I am asking you, therefore, to be more serious about being aware of your environment and keeping a track of developments in a meaningful way.

Flipkart wouldn't have possibly happened had someone at Accel Partners not believed that two young Amazon executives could build Amazon's bête noire in India. Similarly, Oyo probably wouldn't have become a behemoth under Ritesh Agarwal, had somebody at Lightspeed Venture Partners not shown faith in the high school dropout's business acumen. These were risky calls. But VC is a high stakes job, and although the professionals there are rewarded for making the right calls, failure isn't taken to kindly, either. In venture capital, patience and reposing faith in an underdog is crucial to success. Apart from the likes of Flipkart, Oyo and Paytm, there's the instance of Pine Labs and Sequoia India. Pine Labs, an investment Sequoia made about a decade ago, is set to become a unicorn. Sequoia's stake in Pine Labs is likely to be close to a billion dollars post the company's latest fundraise. Bold bets become extremely rewarding in venture capital. Lightspeed India is a case in point. They backed ShareChat at a time when not many people believed that a vernacular social media platform could make a dent in Facebook or Twitter's universe. ShareChat did, and with elan. Its valuation has soared to nearly Rs 3,500 crore, and if things don't turn topsy-turvy, Lightspeed will rake in rich profits.

In the world of private equity, General Atlantic stands out. The firm has invested 2.6 billion dollars in 27 Indian companies and realised 2.4 billion dollars, having exited 13 investments. In the world of private investments, one thing that remains constant—spotting them early and spotting them right. Since 2008, VC has helped Indian entrepreneurs drive value creation at scale, raising over 48 billion dollars in capital from 2,300 unique investors, generating over 130 billion dollars in value. VC-backed companies today contribute over $50 billion to India's GDP, creating over 1.5 million jobs while disrupting traditional sectors and creating new ones.

Early spotting and betting bold can and do pay off. The point to be underlined in bold is that none of these decisions is uninformed. They are well informed and meticulously studied. Never forget that.

When the celebrated futurist Alvin Toffler published Future Shock in 1970, he grouped the world's population into three major categories. Leaving aside a very tiny section which lived on hunting and food gathering, a vast majority of mankind depended on agriculture, living very much as our ancestors did centuries ago. These people, whom Toffler called the people of the past, constituted about 70 per cent of the world's population. The second major group, a little over a quarter of the population, was located in the industrialised societies, marked by mechanisation and mass education. According to Toffler, it constituted the people of the present. Just about two or three per cent of the world's mankind lived at the centres of technological and cultural change such as New York, London and Tokyo, who, he said, were already living the way of the life of the future.

Toffler, however, predicted that "millions more will live tomorrow" this life of the future.

The world has changed drastically since then. Today, 55 per cent of the world's population lives in urban areas. By 2050, the population distribution is expected to be nearly the reverse of the world described by Toffler, with only 32 per cent living in rural areas. More importantly, not only the industrial societies, but even those which were predominantly rural in nature have undergone massive transformation. As Toffler presciently commented, through these transformations, we are not creating a changed society, but a new society.

The transformation into the life of the future has been produced by a web of complex factors, but the role of technology is undeniably central to it. In this complex web, it is difficult to clearly demarcate the cause and effect, for they more often than not, work in loops, feeding each other. Just as technological innovations brought to the people have either produced some changes or reinforced them, at the same time, the changes have produced new business opportunities, which have been turned into profitable ventures by new age companies.

It can be a challenging task for an ordinary individual to keep track of every change, nor is it necessary. What can be done and what should be done instead is to monitor the major changes. Some changes take place slowly over a long period of time whereas others have short term impact. For instance, while climate change has introduced new elements in the corporate world gradually over a number of years and will continue to work its way incrementally, a government policy that provides incentives to new energy technologies that move away from fossil fuels will have an immediate impact on the market. It is important to be aware of both kinds of changes. These changes are so important to businesses and to investors that almost every investment research firm produces its own interpretations and projections every year, if not more frequently.

While these trends influence businesses by changing consumption patterns, businesses themselves are constantly adapting and transforming in response. Apart from these, governance factors regulate the operating environment in which both consumers and industries function.

What follows is a brief description of some of these trends and their possible impacts on businesses, which should concern you as an investor. The analysis brings out the sectors that are slated for a faster pace of growth and more turbulence, as also those which are going to remain steady or even become unattractive over a period of time.

Now that you have gained all this knowledge, do you feel confident enough to make well-informed decisions regarding investment in stocks? Make a list of all the key points you'd like to keep in mind before making your next investment.

Health

Ageing population and changing disease profile

There has been a clear shift towards a greater burden of non-communicable/lifestyle diseases in the past two decades.

Share of non-communicable/lifestyle diseases in disease types.

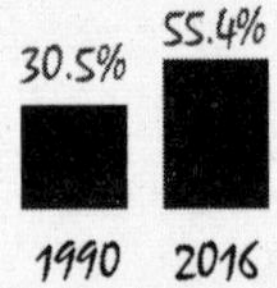

Also known as chronic diseases, the non-communicable diseases such as cardiovascular diseases, cancers, chronic respiratory diseases and diabetes are long-term in nature. The most direct impact of this transition is a significant increase in expenditures of households.

What this means

- Trend of greater reliance on private sector due to inadequate public health infrastructure to strengthen.
- Greater market opportunities for healthcare and pharmaceutical sectors and the suppliers of intermediate products..
- Greater interest in term policies and increasing opportunities for health insurance..

Agriculture

Accounts for **18.8%** of the country's total gross value added.

Problems

- Disporportionate share of working population engaged in farming.
- Low crop yield, falling water levels.
- High farmer debts.
- Land fragmentation.

Likely future trends aimed at making agriculture more efficient

- Migration of workers from agriculture to other sectors.
- Land consolidation (either formal or informal).
- Higher investment in improving crop yield.

What this means

- Greater opportunities for agricultural and biotech companies to improve crop yield.
- Market for farm mechanisation, especially for farming and post-harvest technologies to increase.
- Greater integration of food processing companies in the farming sector once enabling legislation is enacted.

Population

India's population will increase by

468 million until 2062

and then start declining.

Share of youth in population accompanied by an increase in old age population

% share of below 25 years age

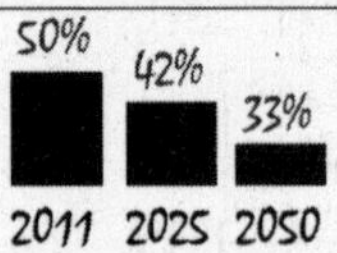

% share of below 50 years age

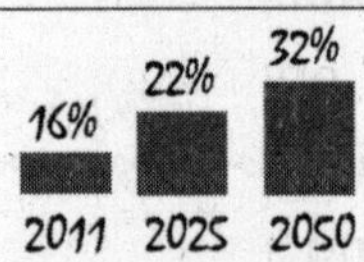

Share of nuclear families in the country's total households is rising rapidly

Rural and urban population of the country are going to be equal by middle of the century

What this means

- More people in the workforce to increase demand for consumer and lifestle products and services.
- Demand for smarter & market-oriented skill providers.
- Smaller families will increase market for family support services.
- Increasing older population will require better medical services.
- Greater demand for urban infrastructure (road, transport, hypermarkets, etc.) and housing

THE JOURNEY TO THE FUTURE

Whether the Indian government's vision to increase the country's economy to 5 trillion dollars by 2025 is realised on time or delayed by a few years, there is no doubt about the country's growth potential. Management think tank McKinsey projects that at a 7 per cent growth trajectory, India's economy will hit the 10 trillion dollars' mark sometime in the 2030s. The optimism is stronger especially since India unlike Brazil and Russia, is not resource dependent for its growth. It is well known that India's growth path has been primarily driven by the services sector, which now accounts for about 58 per cent of the country's GDP, and will continue to do so in the future.

And in this growth scenario, technology is going to play the central role in transforming our lives on a bigger scale and even faster than what we have experienced until now. Much of what used to be in the realm of science fiction is already part of our everyday lives. The future is going to have more of that. From flying taxis, Hyperloop transportation systems, personal robotic assistants, holographic displays through smartphones, routine deliveries by drones, use of 3D printing for construction as well as repairs, to virtual reality in education, the possibilities are endless.